D0882170

MAK

Austrian Museum of Applied Arts
Vienna

Edited by
Peter Noever

Prestel

Edited by Peter Noever

2nd, enlarged edition
© 1995 MAK – Austrian Museum of
Applied Arts, Vienna, and Prestel-
Verlag, Munich and New York

Photographic acknowledgements:
all photos © Gerald Zugmann/MAK
or from the MAK photo archives,
except in the following cases:
© Anna Blau: pp. 173 (bottom), 174
(top); © Manfred Burger/MAK: p. 166
(centre, right and left); © Herbert
Fidler/MAK: p. 175 (top); © Werner
J. Hannappel: p. 164 (bottom);
© Gerhard Koller/MAK: p. 166
(centre, left); © Reinhard Mayr/MAK:
pp. 162 (top), 166 (top), 173 (top);
© Michael Rathmayer/MAK: p. 166
(bottom); © Julius Shulman: p. 170;
© Tim Street-Porter: pp. 169, 171
(top); © Alex Vertikoff: p. 171 (bottom); © Friedrich Zaunrieth/MAK:
p. 163 (bottom right)

Text editors, (1st edition 1993):
Hanna Egger, Rainald Franz
Coordinating editor: *Verena
Formanek*
(2nd edition) *Jessica Beer*

Contributions by
*Barbara Bloom, Eichinger oder
Knechtl, Günther Förg, Gang Art,
Franz Graf, Jenny Holzer, Donald
Judd, Margarete Schütte-Lihotzky,
Manfred Wakolbinger,* and *Heimo
Zobernig*

*Hanna Egger, Birgit Flos, Rainald
Franz, Ulrike Götz, Waltraud
Neuwirth, Peter Noever, Elisabeth
Schmuttermeier, Angela Völker,
Johannes Wieninger,* and *Christian
Witt-Dörring*

New Installations Supervisor (1993):
Verena Formanek
Technical Supervisor:
Wolfgang Glatzner

Prestel books are available worldwide.
Please contact your nearest bookseller
or write to either of the following
addresses for information concerning
your local distributor:
Prestel-Verlag
Mandlstrasse 26, D-80802 Munich,
Germany; Tel. (+49-89) 381 7090;
Fax (+49-89) 38 170935
16 West 22nd Street, New York,
NY 10010, USA; Tel. (212) 6278199;
Fax (212) 6279866

Designed by Dietmar Rautner and
Rainald Schwarz, Munich
Typeset by Max Vornehm GmbH,
Munich
Offset lithography by
Gewa-Repro GmbH, Munich
Printed and bound by
Passavia Druck GmbH, Passau

Printed in Germany
ISBN 3-7913-1472-6
(English edition)
ISBN 3-7913-1468-8
(German edition)

Die Deutsche Bibliothek –
CIP-Einheitsaufnahme

MAK : Austrian Museum of Applied
Arts, Vienna / ed by Peter Noever.
[Contributions: Barbara Bloom …]. –
2., enl. ed. – München ; New York :
Prestel, 1995
  (Prestel museum guides)
  Dt. Ausg. u. d. T.: MAK
  ISBN 3-7913-1472-6
NE: Noever, Peter [Hrsg.]; Bloom,
Barbara; Austrian Museum of Applied
  Arts, Vienna

Contents

Foreword
The "New MAK" – a commission for a new design

If a museum of art does not constantly pursue a course of critical confrontation with the arts, does not recognize contemporary art's modes of perception and viewpoints as a challenge to reassess its own position, it deprives
itself of its very *raison d'être*. The idea of 'preserving' objects and the elements that constitute a collection is inseparably linked to the responsibility
to demonstrate and make visible their contemporary relevance. In order,
therefore, to initiate a process that will gradually dissolve the ideological
contraposition between 'applied' and 'fine' arts, this concept was taken as
the point of departure for a fundamental reorientation that commenced in
1986.

An open and often controversial process involving various forms of presentation (symposia, lectures, conferences, exhibitions, workshops, and
publications) took account of clearly recognizable positions by artists,
philosophers, and scholars, and provided the substance for the changes that
were made. The concept of the 'uniqueness' of an art work, characteristic of
an institution such as the MAK-Austrian Museum of Applied Arts, was con-
fronted by the (transitory) uniqueness of exhibitions containing art works
created especially for this institution (including works by Donald Judd,
Magdalena Jetelová, Walter Pichler, Bernard Rudofsky, Peter Weibel, Hans
Kupelwieser, Chris Burden, and Vito Acconci).

This made it clear that the Museum can no longer remain an isolated
institution consecrated to the historical past if it is to realize its potential and
fulfil its responsibility to provide an active setting for the production of art
and the provision of art education. The incessant change affecting artistic,
cultural, and cultural-political values is the criterion here, the actual challenge.

The urgent necessity of developing an unmistakable identity for the
Museum and clearly defining its social and cultural responsibilities was the
decisive factor for the institution's reorientation with regard to both content
and organization. From the very outset, I considered a comprehensive redesign of all departments to be part of my task. What we started out with was
an architecturally desolate building, indifferent in content and lacking the
appropriate infrastructure. Hence it was necessary critically and progres-
sively to devise a position defining every area anew, and, in the end, effect
reform on every level. The general reconstruction of the building was
intended to substantiate this process in a differentiated form, imbuing the
new values sensitively, yet at the same time clearly signalling its objectives.

With new spatial features, going beyond architectural innovation,
creative contributions (reinstallation of the exhibition galleries), and, not
least, organizational reorientation, the MAK intends to play its part as a
responsible social institution in the formation of cultural values. Corres-
pondingly, the institution should also be seen as a 'museum of art in the
widest sense', whose mission is based on comprehending and defining the
times by taking the contemporary era as its starting point.

Peter Noever
Executive and Artistic Director, MAK

Open House Day, 1992

Unveiling of the gate to the Ring (James Wines/SITE), 1992

Round table discussion on "Positions in Art", 1993, from left to right: Johannes Gachnang, Jan Hoet, Daniela Zyman, James Turrell, Kiki Smith, Kyong Park

Symposium: "The museum as a cultural time machine", 1990, from left to right: Johannes Gachnang, Kaspar König, Alois Müller, Helmut Draxler, Isabella Graw, Eduard Beaucamp

Guided tour of MAK

MINI-MAK on the Open House Day, 1994

MAK discussions on the art of the Stalin era on the occasion of the exhibition "Tyranny of Beauty", 1994, left to right: Vladimir Sorokin, Dimitrij Prigov, Walter Grasskamp, Peter Noever, Peter Gorsen

Opening of the exhibition "Roland Rainer: Vitale Urbanität", 1995, from left to right: Peter Noever, Margarete Schütte-Lihotzky, Roland Rainer, Erhard Busek

History of the Building

The completion of the renovation of the MAK-Austrian Museum for Applied Arts in 1993 meant more than a structural improvement to the building's architectural space. The stimulus for, and the driving force behind this initiative, was the search for a fundamental redefinition of the institution. We seized the opportunity for a radical re-examination of the actual, contemporary potential of what had become a fairly faded establishment, exposing its organizational structure and analysing every level of operations. The renovation and restructuring of the building therefore reflect the philosophy and mode of operation of the entire Museum complex.

Reaching back nearly 130 years, the building's history shows that the Museum was never conceptually completed. Rather, in order to ensure the Museum's continuance as an active and contemporary institution, there were phases over the years in which the desire for reform and a new orientation became particularly urgent. Conflicts between contradictory positions concerning the appropriate role of such a museum were precisely what kept the institution alert and active in the public eye. At issue, among other subjects, were the establishment of a serviceable definition of the term 'applied art', and the relation of the old to the new: how can the old serve as a model without suffocating the new? How can one reconcile traditional expectations dutifully with a desire for openness and experiment? And it was intended all along to make the Museum a contemporary forum for intellectual production, artistic communication, and research.

At the time of its founding in 1864, the 'Austrian Museum for Art and Industry' occupied a unique position among the museums of its day: every other art collection, enriched by centuries of acquisitions, belonged either to the Imperial Court, the Church, or private collectors. The 'Austrian Museum for Art and Industry', on the other hand, did not own a collection. Its founding purpose arose from a scientific concept with a strictly defined, primarily educational role: to stimulate aesthetic sensibilities, and therefore current creative activities, by exposing the public to past works of art; while at the same time documenting current trends in art and industry.

One model for this concept was the South Kensington Museum in London (today the Victoria and Albert Museum), affiliated since 1852 with study collections and a college of applied arts, intended to improve the quality of English arts and crafts. The art historian Rudolf von Eitelberger (1817–85) brought this idea back to Austria with him when he returned from the 1862 London World Fair. He argued that academic attitudes in art were removed from the needs of daily life, and that there was therefore an urgent need to establish a museum for the advancement of aesthetics and manufacturing techniques in designing and producing objects for daily use. 'The Museum's mission is to induce understanding; it should disseminate good taste, and be able to deliver exemplary materials for reproduction in schools and factories, as required.'

The government supported the project, although the Prime Minister, Archduke Rainer, was far more interested in reviving local industry, which had gone into recession after the Revolution of 1848, than in the museum *per se*. On May 12, 1864, the 'Austrian Museum for Art and Industry' was officially opened in the ballroom of the Hofburg (Imperial Palace), with Rudolf von Eitelberger as its first Director. In 1871, the Museum moved into a new building on the Stubenring (designed by the architect Heinrich von Ferstel). The School of Applied Arts, founded in 1868, was to provide the first-ever programme for the systematic training of young artisans, in close co-operation with the Museum. Its new quarters, adjacent to the Museum, were completed in 1877.

The growing collections of objects from every segment of the applied arts soon expanded to include contemporary productions, demonstrating the Museum's effectiveness.

Eitelberger died in 1885, in a period during which Historicism was already beginning to lose its significance. In addition, mechanization and mass production were making traditional manufacturing obsolete.

At the end of the century, the Jugendstil movement brought about a new artistic and social renaissance. The movement's proclamation and demands for a new order were worded similarly to those of Historicism, which had called for a redefinition of atrophied attitudes towards art and society half a century before.

Arthur von Scala (1845–1909), who became director in 1897, reorganized the Museum – in the face of considerable opposition – in the spirit of this new idealism, which also sustained the Vienna Secession. Scala renounced historicizing exhibitions in favour of presentations of the English style and Jugendstil, which was 'particularly provocative to conservatives'. Another of his achievements was to secure the participation of such contemporary artists as Otto Wagner, Felician von Myrbach, Koloman Moser, Arthur Strasser, and Josef Hoffmann in the work of the Museum and the School of Applied Art. According to the Museum's new, altered statutes, the institution's role was to elevate public taste and primarily to further the development of modern, contemporary applied arts through the presentation of selected examples of applied arts, old and new. The acquisition policy

Post unearthed during reconstruction on Weiskirchnerstrasse, 1906

Peter Noever, Terrace plateau in the MAK garden, 1991–1993

was to include historical and modern objects in equal measure. Above all, exhibitions were to make the public more receptive to contemporary production.

Important for the Museum's international significance was the journal *Kunst und Kunsthandwerk* (Arts and Crafts), founded by Scala in 1898, which documented the scientific compilation of the collection and programmatically supported the interests of contemporary art. After the completion of the exhibition tract in Weiskirchnerstrasse in 1909 (designed by architect Ludwig Baumann), Scala retired. In the same year, the School of Applied Arts separated from the Museum to become an independent institute.

The Museum's various collections had gone from serving as prototypes to acting as stimuli. Art was now collected for its own sake, rather than with the intention of amassing prototypical specimens for teaching purposes.

After World War I, the Imperial Fiscal Collection (including Oriental rugs, porcelain, furniture, etc.) came into the Museum's possession in 1919. Richard Ernst (1885–1955), who steered the institution through the war and post-war years until 1950, was able to newly install the permanent collections before the institution was renamed the 'State Museum for Applied Arts' after Austria's 'Anschluss' to the Third Reich (1938–45).

After World War II, the first priority was to repair war damage and solve structural and administrative problems. In 1947, the Museum's programmatic transformation from being an active educational institution to a 'non-sectarian' forum for historical documentation with a particular focus on the art-historical maintenance of the collections became manifest when it was renamed the 'Austrian Museum for Applied Arts'.

The Collections

As the Museum was founded in 1864 without a permanent collection, its holdings had to be assembled from a number of different sources, and focal points had to be established in the process. In line with the Museum's claim to have set up an exemplary collection of prototypical objects relating to art and industry, its first acquisitions were producers' bequests, pattern and specimen collections, and direct commissions by artists and artisans; but there were also a number of 'applied arts' objects, which were otherwise difficult to categorize. The Museum's holdings were built around a nucleus of donated collections and assortments of objects and archives. The eclecticism of the collection therefore reflects the variety of its sources: there are world-renowned collections (rugs, ornamental engravings) alongside industrial prototypes from the Historicist period and individual objects from various sources. Only occasionally did the Museum observe a systematic collection policy.

The inventory lists some 42,000 entries; but this number does not reflect the actual number of objects in the collection, because groups of objects are often recorded under a single inventory number. All in all, the Museum's collection includes between 200,000 and 300,000 individual objects.

The collections are subdivided according to materials, rather than style or epoch. The only exceptions to this are the East Asian Collection, the archive of the Wiener Werkstätte (Vienna Workshops), and the Department of Contemporary Art, established in 1986.

Library and Collection of Works on Paper

The library's original holdings were loans from the founding director, Rudolf von Eitelberger. But the first systematic library catalogue was set up as early as 1869, and the collection grew rapidly through purchases and donations. The library is organized according to subject areas and applications, corresponding to the various collections and departments of the Museum. The original systematic arrangement according to research sources for specific artisan techniques is still preserved today. Both books and graphics are included together in the library. Other specialist libraries that were once arranged similarly (even that of the Victoria and Albert Museum) have since been converted to standard classification systems. Thus, the library remains unique in Europe as a specialized library for the applied arts (with a particular emphasis on Historicism), and, of course, as a constant reference facility for all the Museum's departments.

The library includes collections of manuscripts and manuscript fragments, incunabula, and examples of printing ranging from Late Gothic and Renaissance to Jugendstil, as well as a specialized library for arts and crafts from the eighteenth to the twentieth centuries. The Collection of Works on Paper houses a major collection of decorative engravings from the fifteenth to the eighteenth centuries, the so-called model collection, graphic design, old photographs, drawings from the fifteenth to the twentieth centuries, posters, and woodcuts. At the Vienna World Exhibition of 1873, the Museum acquired sixty full-page illustrations for the Persian novel *Hamza-Nama*, one of the most significant Mogul manuscripts of the sixteenth century. Under the directorship of Hans von Ankwicz-Kleehoven, the furniture drawings and desings from Josef Danhauser's workshop in Wieden were added to the collection in 1931; Ankwicz-Kleehoven also succeeded somewhat later in securing the designs and drawings of the Wiener Werkstätte, as well as the firm's archives, for the Museum.

The library tries to remain absolutely up-to-date in all branches of its specialized field, namely the applied arts, in the broadest sense of the term. Recently, emphasis has been given to contemporary art, architecture, and design, which since 1986 have represented new areas of interest and activity. Two of the library's priorities are to remain as current as possible, and to include a comprehensive selection of international art magazines. The intention, in conjunction with the new reading room, is that the Museum library should develop into a vital intellectual centre.

Furniture and Woodwork

This collection had its origins in loans and legacies. This was how, for example, the classical works of the German cabinetmaker David Roentgen came from the Vienna Polytechnic to the Museum. At the World Fairs in Paris (1867 and 1878) and Vienna (1873), three major pieces of furniture from the English Reform Movement (by Colcutt, Talbot and Pugin) were the first contemporary, international objects the Museum acquired. But commissioned works, more than anything else, contributed to the growth of the collection: professors of the School of Applied Arts, together with Viennese artisans, completed prototypical models, or pieces were ordered and purchased for the Museum's twenty-fifth anniversary. Such works form the core of the furniture collection from the Historicist period.

Arthur von Scala was more interested in practical, functional furniture than in unique model pieces. He brought international furniture from the former Trade Museum, of which he had been the Director, into the collection, and systematically built it up with modern English furniture and stylistic copies. In 1899, he initiated a competition for the furnishing of a living room for a married worker, and the entry that received the second prize was taken into the Museum's collection.

One consequence of the collapse of the monarchy for the Museum was that it received much historic furniture that had formerly belonged to the Imperial Court, including first-rate Austrian furniture of the Empire and Biedermeier periods, as well as the eighteenth century. Also acquired were French Empire and Directoire furniture from the Palffy collection, as well as the oldest piece of furniture in the Museum, a folding chair from the thirteenth century, from the Convent of Admont.

During the Nazi period, English and Austrian furniture pieces from the turn of the century were sold at auction in the Dorotheum, or sold to the National Theatres; in addition, nearly a third of the collection was destroyed in bombing raids. This made the collection's subsequent enrichment by a bequest from Clarisse de Rothschild, a collection of eighteenth-century French furniture, all the more significant. Franz Windisch-Graetz, head of the department from 1954 to 1978, acquired a large part of Hermann Wittgenstein's furnishings, which included furniture from the collections of Koloman Moser and Fritz Waerndorfer, as well as pieces made to designs by Josef Hoffmann and Koloman Moser for the Wiener Werkstätte.

As a consequence of the 'Seating '69' show, the Museum has a wide range of seating furniture from the 1960s. A 1969 donation from a public agency forms the core of the bentwood furniture collection, which was later spectacularly enlarged by the acquisition of the Alexander von Vegesack Collection in 1987–88.

Over the last forty years, the collection's focus and definition have shifted: it is no longer exclusively determined by material (wood), but has rather expanded to include furniture as a typological category in general.

Textiles and Carpets

Specialties of the textiles department are oriental rugs, medieval embroideries, tapestries of the late Middle Ages, liturgical garments, lace, Coptic textiles, Biedermeier fabrics, and textiles of the nineteenth and twentieth centuries. Soon after the Museum's inception, it acquired a collection of medieval liturgical garments, including the Göss Paraments, the Melk Chasuble, and the Salzburg Antependium. Early cornerstones of the fabric collection were a collection of fabrics from the Bock Collection in 1864, dating back to the Middle Ages, and, in the 1880s, a sample of Egyptian Coptic fabrics. In 1891, an exhibition of Oriental carpets at the Trade Museum played a decisive role in the West's rediscovery of knotted carpets; in 1906–7, when the Trade Museum was dissolved, its collection of textiles, carpets, fabrics, and garments from the Far East – including the 'hunting rug' and the only silk Mameluke carpet extant, once owned by the Austrian Imperial Family – came to the MAK-Austrian Museum of Applied Arts.

The lace collection was considerably influenced by a donation from Emilie von Schnapper (1897) and a purchase from Berta von Pappenheim (1935). In 1906, the Museum held the first-ever comprehensive lace exhibition. Around 1900, the Museum acquired a large number of printed and woven English fabrics. As far as local products are concerned, a donation from the firm Johann Backhausen and Sons is worthy of mention. The Museum has a representative collection of Biedermeier fabrics and fabrics of the Historicist movement (fabric collections of the former Polytechnic Institute and the Collection of Viennese Textile Manufacturers). The acquisition of the Wiener Werkstätte archive also filled a significant gap in the textile department.

Glass and Ceramics

The Museum's collection of glass and ceramics covers the whole chronological spectrum from the Middle Ages to the present. Some areas of specialization in the glass collection are Venetian glass, cut and ground glass, *verre doublé*, painted, etched, or engraved glass, iridescent and lustrous glasses, as well as a collection of stained-glass painting. The ceramics collection includes majolica, faience, stoneware, tiled stoves, and porcelain from every major European producer.

Recent years have seen major purchases, including twentieth-century glass from Jugendstil to the 1950s, Vienna porcelain, and other objects.

Islamic and East Asian Art

From the time of the Museum's foundation, its collections were organized according to the materials used; its many objects from the Near and Far East were therefore distributed across a number of different collections. In 1936, a separate department was established for non-European art, with an emphasis on Chinese and Japanese objects from the late eighteenth and nineteenth centuries. The three primary sources of objects for the expanding collection were the two World Fairs of 1867 and 1873, and the first official delegation from the Austro-Hungarian Empire to the Far East, the Austro-Hungarian expedition to Siam, China and Japan in 1869–71 (which included the Museum's future director, Arthur von Scala). The Anton Exner Collection was also a significant addition to the Museum's holdings. After his first East Asian voyage, Exner opened a successful art dealership in Vienna in 1911, featuring East Asian arts and crafts. From his collection, the Museum acquired about 3,500 objects dating from Neolithic times to the beginning of the twentieth century. Particularly worthy of note is the collection of Japanese coloured woodcuts from the eighteenth and nineteenth centuries (in the print collection), which are currently being re-catalogued; the Museum's 10,000 Japanese dyers' stencils are also being prepared for study.

Metalwork

Some of this collection's main emphases are Renaissance jewellery, contemporary jewellery, pewter vessels, Viennese silver, castings (*Galvanos*), metalwork from the Wiener Werkstätte, and tableware.

At first, the Museum acquired castings or *Galvanos* (duplicates cast from the same moulds as the originals), rather than original pieces, the argument being that copies were equally effective as models for study. Bequests from major collectors (such as the Figdor Collection), purchases, and exchanges contributed to the growth of the gold work collection, which specializes in secular objects from the sixteenth to the nineteenth centuries. In 1881, the 'Hall Jewels' – two pearl crowns and a goblet set with precious stones, dating from around 1590 – came into the Museum's possession from the All Saints' Church in the Tyrolean town of Hall. Today, the emphasis of the jewellery collection is on objects from the nineteenth and twentieth centuries.

Purchases of non-precious metals have tended to focus on artisan works by journeymen or masters from past centuries, such as keys, locks, the guild trademarks, graveyard crosses, and balcony railings. Also in the collection are a wealth of Austrian, English, and French pieces dating from around 1900 – objects directly purchased from the artists or manufacturers themselves. Today, these form an important part of the Jugendstil collection. Contemporary Austrian jewellery has currently found powerful new momentum. One of the collection's functions will be to exhibit and document these new trends.

The Wiener Werkstätte (Vienna Workshops) Archive

The complete archive of the Wiener Werkstätte artists' association (1903–1932) was acquired in 1955 at the urging of the library's Director at the time, Hans von Ankwicz-Kleehoven. The archive encompasses artists' drawings and designs for various materials, fashion designs, pattern books, volumes of photographs, files of correspondence, graphic design, newspaper clippings, and design sketches for fabric, glass, ceramics, metal objects, jewellery, furniture and leatherwork, postcards, printed fabric patterns, wallpaper, and books of wallpaper patterns (currently in the textiles collection). The production process of all the various artisan and manufacturing trades practised by a Viennese firm can be reconstructed from the archive with uncommon clarity and precision. The cataloguing of this archive, which is far and away the Museum's most extensive collection, is not yet complete. Since the 1967 exhibition 'Wiener Werkstätte – Modern

Artisanship from 1903–1932' at the MAK, a number of publications and exhibitions have begun systematically to examine the work of this association of artists and craftsmen.

Contemporary Art

This collection was established in 1986 in a deliberate attempt to support the Museum's programmatic reorientation towards contemporary art. In the age of mass production, objects of applied art are primarily interesting as cultural and historical objects, but can hardly be taken as models for contemporary aesthetic production. A move towards a comprehensive evaluation of contemporary design is the so-called 'Design Info Pool', currently being set up as a long-term research project, and intended to include all relevant data about designers currently working in Austria. Neither applied arts nor design are in themselves adequate role models or stimuli for contemporary debate. Art itself is a much more powerful ignition force. The Museum's collection does not include painting; instead, it houses works on the boundaries between disciplines, works with a spatial dimension, installations, and architecture in the broadest sense of the term.

Gate to the Ring, 1992, Entrance to the Minerva Bookshop at the MAK, by James Wines/ SITE

Above: *Excavating the columned Main Hall in the Stubenring wing of the MAK.* Below: *Press conference with Peter Noever in February 1987 in the MAK's furniture depository*

Reconstruction

In February of 1986, I was entrusted with the Directorship of the MAK-Austrian Museum of Applied Arts. At the time, the Museum building was in a desolate state of repair, and its conception and programme had been dramatically neglected. A redefinition of the whole institution on every level was vitally needed. Unlike other museums, the MAK has never defined itself as an institution devoted solely to the preservation and administration of museum objects, but has always tried, in accordance with its mandate, to engage in an energetic confrontation with the present. To give life to this strong sense of the contemporary, the Museum had to be completely reorganized, both physically and structurally. Only a fundamental reorientation would enable the Museum to become a truly vital centre for contemporary art.

Since reforming an institution from the inside out is a highly complex undertaking, experts were called in to develop – in symposia and research studies – positions and analyses on the issue of reform and the Museum's role within a larger social context. 'The Collections and Reorganization', a catalogue of architectural measures and an evaluation of the current use of space, was commissioned as early as April 1986. This study not only yielded the relevant data and prerequisites for the Museum's restoration, but also became a basis of discussion for Vienna's other national museums, which were waiting for a signal from the state in order to begin their own desperately-needed renovations. In July of 1987, the Cabinet of Ministers approved the first 'Museums Billion', one billion Schillings earmarked for the restoration of Austria's national museums. The financial means for the renovation plans were thereby guaranteed.

Principal Architectural Measures

1990 saw the opening of the underground storage area beneath the Museum garden: its two floors provided 3,400 square metres of storage for the Museum's collections, providing ideal conservation conditions.

By excavating the cellar beneath the columned Main Hall, the Museum acquired another underground storey for the new study collection (1,960 square metres).

The renovation enlarged the exhibition spaces for the permanent collection in the building on the Stubenring to nearly 2,400 square metres, which includes the MAK gallery for temporary exhibitions by contemporary artists. The gallery spaces opening off the Main Hall are again used to exhibit the permanent collection. By placing a ceiling over the gallery for Oriental carpets, a new reading room for the library was created, which was furnished by the architects Ursula Aichwalder and Hermann Strobl.

With the renovations, the exhibition hall in the Weiskirchnerstrasse building, measuring 3,000 square metres over two storeys, is one of the largest in Vienna. Some of the workshops have moved up from the cellar into the attic, which has been supplied with optimal technical facilities.

The lecture hall on the top floor has been converted into an audiovisual presentation room. In the foyer, the MAK Design Shop measures 80 square metres, and sells products from the MAK's design line, as well as works by contemporary designers. Altogether, the conversions have provided the Museum with 5,000 square metres of additional space.

More immediately obvious for the Museum's new identity than the conversion and restoration work are the artistic signs and manifestations on the building's exterior. The 'Gate to the Garden' (Walter Pichler, 1990) provides access to the newly-open free space of the Museum garden, which was first integrated into the Museum's complex in 1909, and has today again become an indispensable part of the MAK's facilities. The concrete terraced plateau (Peter Noever, 1991–93) is at once the border, limit, and extension of the garden, and also provides a connection with the adjacent building, the School of Applied Arts. A freight elevator with access to the storage area in the basement and the various exhibition levels is located in the connecting tract (Sepp Müller, 1991) between the building on the Stubenring and the exhibition hall on Weiskirchnerstrasse.

Next to the main entrance of the Stubenring building is the MAK bookshop (Sepp Müller, 1992), built on 30 square metres, 12 metres high, with various interior levels for presentation. The New York architect James Wines/SITE transplanted an element of the original façade, with a window, from the historic building to a space on the pedestrian walkway as a 'Gate to the Ring' (1992). This piece of narrative architecture in Vienna could be understood as an embodiment of the Museum's new opening outwards and unfolding. Another opening toward the city is the MAK Café on the Stubenring (Hermann Czech, 1993), accessible from the Ring and the Museum, which also opens onto the Museum garden.

Operational Reorganization

The reorientation of the institution's infrastructure was carried out simultaneously with the physical alterations (as the Museum was never closed during the building period). Once again, it was two survey reports which served as the main impetus for change. Christian Reder's 1987 'Services Study' discussed services the Museum could provide on a free-enterprise

Walter Pichler, Gate to the garden, 1990

Reconstruction of the exhibition room for twentieth-century architecture and design

basis to increase both its effectiveness and its income; the report helped to hasten the introduction of partial legal autonomy for national museums, and was approved by Parliament on 1 July, 1989. Without this law, giving museums the power to undertake autonomous free-enterprise activities, significant changes to the infrastructure would have been impossible. Reder's second study, 'New Collection Policies and Operational Structures' (1991), clarified the various working levels of the organization and served as a departure point for organizational analysis and restructuring.

'Tradition and experiment' are the twin principles setting out the Museum's two main tasks: on the one hand, the scientific preservation, expansion, and presentation of the institution's unique collection; on the other, an active and risk-taking dialogue with contemporary artistic trends. Analysis made it clear that these two areas must be given separate but equal priority. Separating long-range tasks and temporary activities within these two departments enables the whole organization to plan and operate more effectively.

'Collections, Science and Research', the Museum's collection-related division, is responsible for building up information and document archives, for defining an acquisition policy with definite areas of focus, and for putting out publications about the collections, presenting new subjects and new theories to be pursued. The second department, 'Exhibitions and Events', organizes exhibitions, symposia, discussion and lecture series, workshops, conferences, films, and other interdisciplinary forms of dialogue to be developed. The department of 'Central Services' focuses on personnel and finance. The position of Chief Curator was also introduced into the organizational hierarchy.

Innovations and new emphases now have to be introduced into the daily running of the Museum; they should in no case be seen as rigid prescriptions which might inhibit new, interesting, necessary growth. The Museum's organization remains in a vacillating balance between the productive chaos of an experiment in transition and a new maximally structured order. All through the restructuring process, these radical efforts have given rise to similarly demanding formulations and challenges: that a museum with a contemporary orientation towards new projects should remain committed to the presentation of its traditional collections; that traditional art can only be apprehended in a meaningful way if it is interpreted by means of contemporary art; that the new has to be activated by the old, and vice versa. How conclusive or productive such perspectives really are can only be ascertained over time in the Museum's daily operations.

Artistic Intervention

The decision to invite contemporary artists to reinstall the MAK's permanent collection and redesign the gallery spaces was therefore the first experiment to be realized in the course of the Museum's search for a new identity. Here, for the first time, one can sense what the notion of fruitful confrontation between traditional collections and new artistic trends signifies. A conscious decision was made not to have architects design any of the spaces. This experiment promises different new approaches, perspectives, and viewpoints in relation to the objects in the collections, and supplies the objects with fresh, contemporary legibility in a way that re-educates our eyes and our perceptions towards the specific sensitivities and strengths of the individual materials.

Objective display is impossible in a museum; to display is at once to present, to interpret, and to evaluate. The MAK chose to realize the viewpoints of ten significant contemporary artists, who reinstalled the permanent collection after intense collaboration and long discussions with the responsible curators.

The permanent collection is arranged in chronological order – not, however, with the intention of 'covering' each stylistic epoch as completely as possible, but rather of introducing the Museum's highlights, its particularly interesting and unique objects. (In the study collection, on the other hand, the Museum's traditional arrangement according to materials has been preserved in a tight, orderly form of presentation.) Working with colours, special lighting installations, electronic text displays, special display cases, pedestals, and special perceptual alienation effects, the artists found a variety of spatial solutions for 'their' respective rooms. Particularly striking was the fact that, while pursuing their highly personal strategies, they carried out their tasks with such a respect and understanding for the objects that it always remained unmistakable that displaying these objects was their primary motivation, and there was no suspicion of self-presentation. One has to subject oneself to the qualities of the rooms and decide for oneself whether or not this concept has proved to be right; whether the artistic involvement adds a new dimension to contemporary interpretation; whether it actually contributes to the complexity and multiplicity to which the Museum aspires.

The artists themselves responded energetically to the unusual task, albeit with varying degrees of enthusiasm and periods of intense frustration in the process. Donald Judd, for example, ended up thinking it would have been better to install the Dubsky Chamber underground, partly because he had trouble with any kind of museum installation; and Barbara Bloom committed the sacrilege of mentioning the bentwood furniture – the serial, almost minimalistic variations of which she made clearly visible – in the same breath as the mass-produced furniture of IKEA.

All of the rooms have been the subject of much discussion. But in fact, the Museum could not ask for anything better than to spark off a radical, critical debate about the relation of old to new, about how to bring old, traditional spaces into the present day and into correspondence with the work of contemporary artists.   *Peter Noever*

Installation by Vito Acconci for the exhibition 'The City Inside Us', 1993, in the MAK's Main Hall

Romanik
Gotik
Renaissance

Romanesque
Gothic
Renaissance

Romanico
Gotico
Rinascimento

Designing artists:
Günther Förg
Display cases: Matthias Esterhazy

Curator: Angela Völker

When the MAK asked me to instal the Romanesque, Gothic, and Renaissance room, there was for me only one possible solution – to link our time with the past. The pieces on display consist of the Göss paraments, various majolica pieces from the Renaissance, and a few items of furniture. For conservation reasons, almost all of these have to be protected by glass display cases.

The idea for the design is based on two direct interventions: firstly, providing a coloured frame for the walls, and secondly, redesigning the display cases. For the first intervention, a connection had to be made between the delicate colouring of the Göss paraments, the strong, unfaded colours of the majolica, here dominantly ultramarine and ochre, and the room's ceiling colour. I decided on a light cobalt blue, which has a certain festive quality, but is also discordant with the colour of the ceiling.

The design of the display cases was carried out with Matthias Esterhazy, the goal being to arrive at a classic display case that would also reflect our own time. Objects such as the Göss paraments are shown with natural folds, and others, such as the portable writing desks, at a natural height. An exception to this is the raised presentation of a small vessel for vinegar and oil, which is shown as a single item in a relatively large display case.   *Günther Förg*

Much medieval handicraft has been preserved in churches and monasteries, and from these it has occasionally made its way to museums. This is the case with the most significant Romanesque works in the Museum, the so-called 'Göss Paraments' and the folding stool from Admont.

The furniture and ceramics of the fifteenth and sixteenth centuries from northern and southern Europe that are presented here illustrate specific regional characteristics, and the survival of stylistic features over long periods. Austrian handicrafts of the fifteenth century, for example, are still considered as Gothic. Although the Renaissance began in Italy during the first quarter of the fifteenth century, its influence was only felt north of the Alps from the second half of the century, continuing into the early seventeenth century, as the richly inlaid bureau cabinet from Augsburg shows.

Italian majolica vessels illustrate the ceramic ornamentation and painting of the High Renaissance. Imitation of the classical style is seen here, as well as the way in which pictorial representations were successfully transferred into a different medium.   *Angela Völker*

Antependium
Linen, silk embroidery
Inv. no. T 6902

Depicted in the medallions: Annunciation to the Virgin, Virgin enthroned with Child, the Three Kings. Below left, alongside the central medallion: Kunigunde; to her right, St. Adala, founder of the Convent at Göss, with a model of the church.

Paraments
from the Convent at Göss

Göss (Styria), mid-13th century
Linen, silk embroidery
Inv. no. т 6.902 – т 6.906, acquired from
the Convent at Göss in 1908

The Museum's collection of textiles
includes a wealth of medieval religious textiles, the most significant of which are the
paraments from the Benedictine convent at
Göss – the only surviving ensemble of
church robes preserved from such an early
period (ca. 1260). The priest wore the
chasuble and cope, the deacon and subdeacons the dalmatic and tunic. The
antependium was an ornamental covering
for the front of the altar table. This assortment of paraments can easily be recognized
as an ensemble on the basis of its shared
technique, colouring, and style. Some serious alterations made during the course of

the centuries, as well as the free form of the
ornamentation, give the vestments a particularly colourful and unusually decorative appearance today.

Kunigunde, Abbess of the Convent
from 1239 to 1269, donated the vestments
and, together with other canonesses, prepared them herself. The images and
inscriptions on the antependium, chasuble, cope, and dalmatic are evidence of this
quite unusual procedure for the Middle
Ages. The scenic representations in the
medallions were probably designed by a
painter using ink on the cloth. The nuns
then embroidered the scene with coloured
silk, using various types of stitching. The
originally concealed sketches can be seen
quite well in places where the embroidery
is damaged. The ornamentation and pattern, by contrast, were produced without
any precise design, and this explains their
unorthodox distribution.

Cope
Linen, silk embroidery
Inv. no. т 6903

Depicted in the medallions: Maria suckling the Christ Child, surrounded by the emblems of the four Evangelists: eagle (John), angel (Matthew), lion (Mark), and bull (Luke). Beneath the large medallion: Kunigunde with a nun, originally part of the chasuble.

Chasuble
Linen, silk embroidery
Inv. no. т 6904

The chasuble, like the cope, originally consisted of a semi-circle, which was closed in front and embroidered. Today's much smaller form derives from the eighteenth century. Back: Christ enthroned with the emblems of the four Evangelists, and below them nine angels in three rows of stilted-arch arcades. Front: Crucifixion, and beneath it eight Apostles in two rows of stilted arches, corresponding to the angels on the back.

Leaf of a table
Swabia, late 15th century
Cherry wood, painted
Inv. no. H 255/1871

Folding stool
Salzburg (?), early 13th century
Pear wood, carved and painted; leather
seating added later
Inv. no. H 1705/1935

Cabinet
South Germany, Augsburg (?), last third of
the 16th century
Maple wood, veneered, marquetry in
various types of wood; etched and gilded
ironwork
Inv. no. H 218/1871

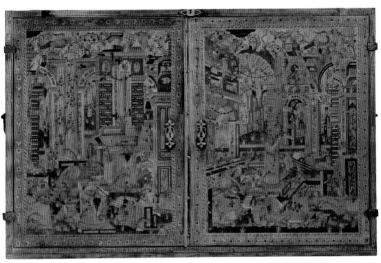

Vessel for vinegar and oil
Known as 'Medici porcelain'
Proto-porcelain, silver
Height: 16.4 cm
Inv. no. KE 8050

Majolica pitcher with grotesque handle
Urbino, 16th century
Height: 33.7 cm
Inv. no. KHM 3141

**Barock
Rokoko
Klassizismus**

**Baroque
Rococo
Classicism**

**Barocco
Rococò
Neoclassico**

Designing artist: **Donald Judd**

Curator: Christian Witt-Dörring

I was doubtful about the idea of artists making installations of earlier objects; I am still doubtful. I think installation should be the responsibility of the curators of the objects, although I continue to be critical of the generally artificial way in which objects are installed. To have artists make such installations is likely to perpetuate devious installation. I accepted the problem as a favour to the museum, and I accepted as a premise for myself that I would not contradict the judgement of the curator responsible, Christian Witt-Dörring. I think we did our best. The museum's premise, the installation's set fact, was that the Dubsky room, originally a room in a palace, had to be reconstructed in a much larger room of the museum. I was told there was no alternative. The room could be remade either in one of the corners of the exhibition room, leaving an awkward right angle for the other furniture, or it could be remade in the centre of the room, leaving a symmetrical space and possibly establishing a room within a room – a good idea. I asked that this be done. The Dubsky room is too large and is awkward, but placing it in the centre was the right decision. The room and most of the other furniture were made in the eighteenth century for the aristo-cracy. The room's grandeur is uncertain, and therefore excessive. It is uneasy; Chardin is not uneasy. All architecture and most installations are now uneasy. Why is Chardin simple, strong and easy? The separate pieces of furniture are placed symmetrically, usually in pairs, usually opposite each other. A rectangu-lar space usually determines this. The positioning of the furniture was also care-fully decided with regard to the size, colour, and type of each piece. I asked for part of the moulding under the ceiling of the large room to be repeated around the exterior of the Dubsky room, to further incorporate it into the eighteenth century space made in the nineteenth century, and to reduce the excessive gen-erality of its exterior. This is a small, uneasy room uneasily placed in a large, doubly uneasy room. I think it should be in the basement. But Witt-Dörring and I did our best, uneasily. *Donald Judd*

The MAK's collections contain some splendid examples of eighteenth-century cabinet-making. The emphasis in the collection is on pieces from the cultural realm encompassing Austria, Germany, and France. These witness to the tre-mendous typological, technical, and formal developments that took place during the course of the eighteenth century. The bureau cabinet, with its origins in the seventeenth century, is gradually replaced as a prestigious furniture item by the writing desk, the southern German form of which is known as a 'tabernacle cabinet'. In France, the chest of drawers develops as a new kind of case furniture providing interior storage space for the living area, a reaction to the growth of the private sphere and the increasing desire for comfort. Forms of writing furniture that arise include the basic desk and the cylinder desk. The surface decoration of furniture becomes more varied, and is used to meet novel requirements and fashions (wooden and Boulle marquetry, lacquer, porcelain, etc.). Interior design itself becomes more uniform with the development of mobile and immobile furnishings. Furniture enters into decorative unity, and often even structural unity, with the room. The porcelain room from the Dubsky Palace in Brno eloquently documents this, as well as marking the beginning of porcelain production in Vienna, from 1719 onward.   *Christian Witt-Dörring*

Bureau Cabinet
Neuwied am Rhein, 1776
Design and manufacture: David Roentgen
Clock: signed 'Kintzing à Neuwied'

Maplewood stained brown, rosewood and myrtle, variously coloured woods, gilded bronze fittings
Inv. no. H 269/1871

Cabinet
Cheb (Czech Republic), 1723
Design and manufacture: Nikolaus
Haberstumpf
Signed: 'Johann Nickolaus Haberstumpf
fecit 1723 kunstdischler und mohler in
Eger' [cabinet-maker and painter in Eger
(the German name for Cheb)]
Veneered ebony, relief marquetry and mar-
quetry in various types of wood
Inv. no. H 1760/1941

Chest of drawers
Paris, 1778
Design and manufacture: Jean-Henri
Riesener
Signature: 'J. H. RIESENER'
Amaranth wood, marquetry in various
woods, gilded bronze fittings, marble top
(serancolin)
Inv. no. H 1969/1948
Gift of Clarisse de Rothschild, in memory of
Dr. Alfons de Rothschild

Chest of drawers
Paris, ca. 1745/49
Lacquer (China, 18th century, with Euro-
pean additions), gilded bronze fittings
(with a crowned 'C' stamp), marble top
(brèche d'Alepe)
Inv. no. H 1968/1948
Gift of Clarisse de Rothschild, in memory of
Dr. Alfons de Rothschild

Small table
Vienna, 1769
Design and manufacture: Wilhelm
Gottlieb Martitz
Signature: 'W. Martitz In Wienn Den 19
August Anno 1769'
Gilded bronze, silver leaf, marble
Inv. no. LHG 1412/1973
Lent by the Creditanstalt-Bankverein

**Porcelain chamber from the
Dubsky Palace in Brno**
Vienna, ca. 1740
Inv. no. KE 6201/1912

Around 1700, it became fashionable in
Europe to decorate rooms as so-called
'porcelain chambers'. Initially, only European faience was available, but as time
went on its place was taken by Chinese
imports and, from 1700, by Japanese porcelain. The porcelain chamber from the
Dubsky Palace in Brno is one of the first
rooms to be decorated with European
porcelain.

The decoration of the room can be
traced as far back as the years following
1724, from the coat of arms of the Czobor
von Szent-Mihály family over the trumeau.
At this period, Duchess Maria Antonia of
Czobor, Frau auf Göding, born Princess of
Liechtenstein, purchased in Brno what

Library table
Vienna, ca. 1730
Walnut and maple, veneered
Inv. no. H 1185/1909

was later to become the Dubsky Palace. The porcelain from the Vienna manufactory Du Paquier (1718–44) also dates from this period. Studies of the room's fixed wall panelling, and the fact that, even in Brno, the fireplace had no smoke outlet and therefore could not be used, show that the decoration must have been originally designed for a different location, still unknown, and was only later adapted to the smaller dimensions of the Brno palace. However, there is a discrepancy in time that has still not been clarified between the examples of early Viennese porcelain, produced prior to 1730, and the ornamentation of the wall panelling and some of the furniture, the earliest dating for which can only be to the 1740s.

In 1745, the palace came into the possession of Johann Georg von Piati, whose son Emanuel Piati von Tirnowitz inherited it in 1762. The family's coat of arms was formerly painted over that of the Czobor, and was only removed in 1912 when the room was purchased by the Museum. The addition of paintings, and of a wall-clock signed by the Brno master clockmaker Sebastian Kurz, also dates from the Piati period, around 1790. The palace received its current name when Emanuela von Piati, the daughter of Johann Georg, married Franz Dubsky von Trebomyslic in 1805. Later additions of porcelain from the Herend Porcelain Manufactory (founded in 1839), and items from the Vienna Porcelain Manufactory dated 1847, show that extensive restoration and readaptation of the room must have been carried out around 1850. The chairs, as well as the console table on the long wall and the sofa table, also very probably date from this period.

Table centrepiece from Zwettl Monastery

Vienna, 1768 and earlier
Glazed, unpainted porcelain; the support consists of nine parts standing on low legs, and is set with mirrors 428 x 51 cm with 60 figure groups, inidivual figures, and vases
Inv. no. KE 6823

The centrepiece was ordered on the occasion of the golden jubilee of the ordination of Abbot Rayner I. Kollmann of Zwettl Monastery. The 'whole dessert in three crates' was transported to Zwettl by carriage in May 1768 and presented to the Abbot at his jubilee celebration. For this occasion Joseph Haydn composed his 'Applausus', which may be related to the table centrepiece, as the female allegories of the virtues that appear on it also feature in Haydn's composition as female voices.

Bratlkoch (a Viennese market cry)
Marks: 'Bindenschild' in underglaze blue, stamped embosser's mark 'P' (= Anton Peyer), '5' (inscribed)
Height: 9.4 cm
Inv. no. KE 6823/18

Wigmaker (Perückenmacher)
Marks: 'Bindenschild' in underglaze blue, stamped embosser's mark '0' (= Dionysius Pollion), '5' (inscribed)
Height: 9 cm
Inv. no. KE 6823/22

The Production of Porcelain
(Die Porzellanerzeugung)
(Central group)
Mark: 'Bindenschild' in underglaze blue
Height: 33.5 cm
Inv. no. 6823/6

**Barock
Rokoko**

**Baroque
Rococo**

**Barocco
Rococò**

Designing artist: **Franz Graf**

Curator: Angela Völker

A design intention = states of affairs. The wealth of appearances. The legacy of those who were here before us = the form of actions, our inheritance = memory: museums are also, like cemeteries, our quiet bliss: because the nature of the encounter also gives rise to understanding: it seems there can be no truth concerning this, but only original, brilliant works: silence is the word extinct. Because the same thing once meant something else: because the essence of things is forever dead, and its material properties maintain this expansion into a different world: because a past exists that the living individual can reach into and at least the possibility is hinted at of coming to an end through oneself and beyond with the early ***** appearance.   *Franz Graf*

The MAK's collection of lace, and its holdings of glassware – especially Venetian glass – are today considered among the finest and most varied in the world. Even in the Baroque period, Venetian glasswork was particularly treasured, and both men and women spent vast sums on the sumptuous lace decoration that fashion demanded.

While glass-making is one of the oldest handicraft techniques in the world, the history of lace-making only begins in the late Renaissance period, probably in Italy. A distinction is made between needlepoint lace and bobbin lace, but combinations of the two techniques are often seen. Florence, and later Venice and Milan, were the centres of Italian lace-making in the sixteenth and seventeenth centuries, before lace-making in France and Flanders began during the eighteenth century.

Venice was the centre of European glass-making from the Middle Ages onwards. Around 1500, Venetian glass-makers succeeded in producing clear, colourless glass. Glassblowing spread from Venice across the whole of Europe. In the north, centring on Bohemia and Silesia, there was a preference for harder glass that could be decorated with relief or intaglio engraving, or glass decorated with enamel, *Schwarzlot*, or gold.

This presentation of glasswork and lacework is not based only on art-historical criteria, but also on the visual effects of the materials – their 'transparency', material delicacy, and the virtuosity of the craftsmanship involved in their production – which may today be the aspect of them that arouses the greatest admiration.   *Angela Völker*

Broad collar with figures and ornamentation
Italy, second half of the 16th century
Needlepoint lace with bobbin-lace edging, linen yarn
Inv. no. T 8596/1932

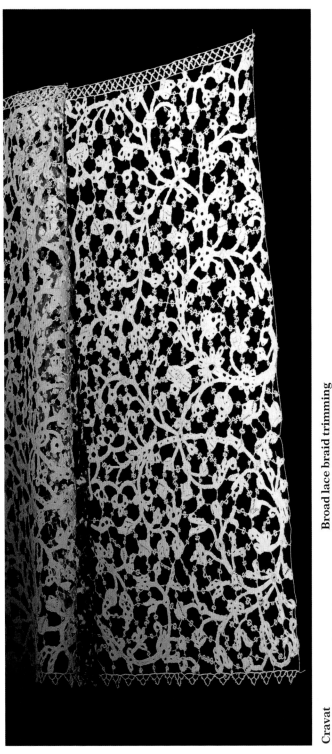

Cravat
Brussels, first quarter of the 18th century
Bobbin lace, linen yarn
Inv. no. T 3708/1884

Broad lace braid trimming
Venice, ca. 1700
Needlepoint lace with bobbin-lace edging,
linen yarn
Inv. no. T 10073/1935

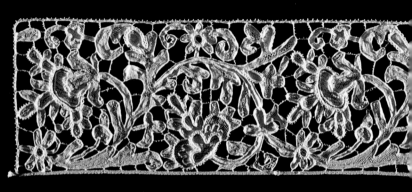

Baroque, Rococo

Lace shawl
(christening shawl?)
First half of the 17th century
Needlepoint lace, coloured silk, metal
threading
Inv. no. T 3064/1878

Fitted relief lace
Venice, mid-17th century
Needlepoint lace with bobbin-lace edging,
linen yarn
Inv. no. T 10073/1906

Cylindrical vessel with lid
Venice, 16th century
Diagonal threaded pattern of smooth and
twisted threads
Height: 35 cm
Inv. no. KHM 3311

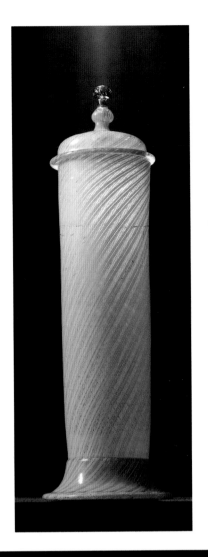

Beaker
Bohemia, beginning of the 18th century
Glass and three dice made of bone
Height: 9.5 cm
Engraved clusters of flowers and foliage
tendrils on the upper, tendrilled frieze in
gold on the cemented joint of the 18-sided
cut-glass base. On the base of the beaker, a
medallion with a leaping stag, gold on red.
Inv. no. GL 2569

Kuttrolf (sprinkler)
Venice, 16th century
Bottle with two white threading patterns
Height: 30.1 cm
Bulb-shaped bottle, with a hollow projec-
tion emerging from the base. Long, thin,
curving neck. Broader mouth, with spout.
Inv. no. KHM 3293

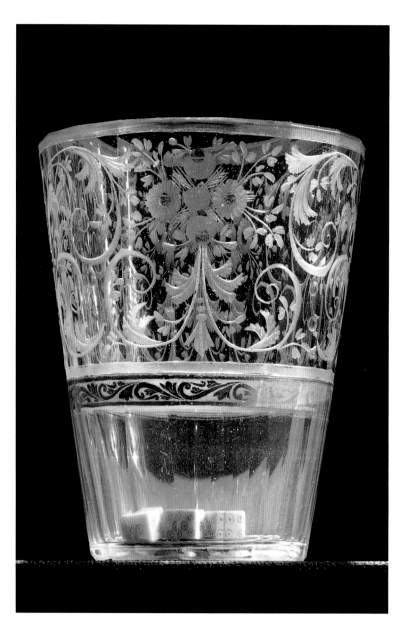

Goblet

Bohemia, 17th century
Height: 10.5 cm; length: 13.5 cm; width:
4.5 cm
Stem glass with a flat base and boat-shaped
calyx, with engraved depictions of a landscape on the base, two gods driving across
the sea on the calyx, and a coat of arms at
the prow.
Inv. no. GL 1815

Goblet with lid

Bohemia, 18th century
Glass, engraved coat of arms of Duke Christoph Wilhelm von Thürhein
Height: 10.5 cm; diameter: 11.5 cm
(mouth), 13 cm (base)
Goblet with faceted shaft, with gold and
ruby threading. Coat of arms medallion
with foliage and ribboning. On the lid,
further engraved foliage and ribboning; the
knob of the lid continues the gold and ruby
threading of the shaft.
Inv. no. GL 172

**Empire
Biedermeier**

Empire Style
Biedermeier

*Stile impero
Biedermeier*

Designing artist:
Jenny Holzer

Curator: Christian Witt-Dörring

I never have liked museum labels and brochures. I wanted to find another system to present information about the collection and about the times in which the objects were made. I tried to think of an appealing way to show a super-abundance of text on Biedermeier and Empire. I chose electronic signs with large memories to talk about why what was produced for whom. The signs display the predictable facts, and softer material such as personal letters of the period. Because some people hate to read in museums, I placed the signs near the ceiling so they can be ignored. To encourage people who might read, I varied the signs' programmes and included special effects. For serious, exhausted readers, I provided an aluminium mock-Biedermeier sofa on which to sit. I also rearranged the furniture, silverware, glassware, and porcelain, as would any good housewife. *Jenny Holzer*

Sofa, model no. 57
Vienna, ca. 1825/1830
Design and manufacture:
Danhauser'sche Möbelfabrik
Cherry wood, solid and veneered
on softwood; original upholstery
reproduced
Inv. no. H 2627/1983

A heterogeneous mass of consumers arose during the first half of the nineteenth century, something never previously seen in Austrian cultural history. With the effects of the Industrial Revolution and the growing cultural, social, and economic strength of the middle classes, it became both possible and necessary to produce differentiated products for these consumers. Items that had previously only been available to a small circle of consumers could be put at the disposal of the more general public. Besides the wide variety of tastes, the range of products on offer was therefore also marked by a subtle gradation from expensive luxury items to cheap substitutes. A generally understood language for materials and forms sprang up, which was no longer specific to any particular social stratum, but instead determined by financial factors. What was displayed was no longer as symbolic in character, relating instead to real people, things, and events.

The selection of objects displayed here therefore shows, alongside outstanding achievements of Austrian art and craft production, above all the variety of designs and materials used for everyday commodities during the Empire and Biedermeier period. The explosion of richly varying forms is demonstrated by a series of variations in chairs, porcelain cups with a limitless range of moods, glasses conveying all sorts of information, and silverware pieces with designs ranging in character from abstract to decorative.   *Christian Witt-Dörring*

Desk
Vienna, ca. 1825
Cherry wood, solid and veneered, wood stained black; tin insets with green lacquer; foot pad renewed
Inv. no. H 2558/1940

Night table
Vienna, ca. 1825/1830
Cherry wood, solid and veneered; Kelheim top; brass fittings
Inv. no. H 3042/1989

Bureau cabinet
Vienna, ca. 1815
Mahogany, wood stained black, carved limewood, partly painted black and with verd-antique finish, partly gilded and bronzed; gilt brass and bronze fittings, partly solid and pressed; inside, maple, grained wood, stained red
Inv. no. H 2027/1955

Inkstand

With depiction of the first giraffe in Vienna
Viennese porcelain, signed and dated:
'Schufried 828' (i.e. Jakob Schufried 1828)
Tray, inkpot and sand-castor
Tray: diameter 20.8 cm; inkpot: height
9.6 cm; sand-castor: height 7.8 cm
Inv. no. KE 240
From the estate of the Vienna Porcelain
Manufactory

Kettle

Vienna, 1820
Josef Kern
Silver
Inv. no. GO 1333/1907

Cup with handle

Vienna, 1811

Marks: 'Bindenschild' in underglaze blue, mark (inscribed), production year '810' (?) (stamped), turner's number '21' (i.e. Ignaz Winter), form number '104' (impressed), painter's number '14' (probably J. Herold, Jr.), gold painter's number '130' (i.e. Karl Hinterberger)

Lip: height 7.4 cm; handle: length 9.2 cm

Inv. no. KE 1087

From the estate of the Vienna Porcelain Manufactory

Cup with handle

Vienna, 1811

Marks: 'Bindenschild' in underglaze blue, production year '811' (stamped), turner's number '36' (i.e. Anton Landskron), form number '104' (impressed), mark (inscribed)

Lip: height 7.5 cm; handle: length 9.9 cm

Inv. no. KE 10100

Items from a breakfast service
With views of Imperial palaces and gardens, based in part on older engravings
Viennese porcelain, ca. 1818
Signed: 'Schufried 1818' (i. e. Jakob Schufried)
Vessel with handle: height 22 cm; cup with handle: height 9.6 cm; saucer: diameter 14.5 cm; sugar bowl: height 10.9 cm
Inv. no. KE LKH 267

Tumbler

Vienna, ca. 1830

Tumbler flaring upward over fluted base, with enamel decoration and gilding. In a square, bordered field: 'Place de la Bibliothèque Imp.le et Roy.le et la Statue Joseph II à Vienne' (Anton Kothgasser, Vienna)

Height: 12 cm; diameter: 9.5 cm (top), 7.4 cm (bottom)

Inv. no. GL 2365

Beaker
Vienna, 1812
Cylindrical tumbler with gilding and trans-
parency painting of Karlovy Vary
(Karlsbad), oak wreath, fly, 'Mon Paradies',
on the base: 'Charles'
Signed: 'G. Mohn, Vienne, 1812'
Height: 9.8 cm; diameter: 7.1 cm
Inv. no. GL 2823

**Historismus
Jugendstil**

**Historicism
Art Nouveau**

**Storicismo
Jugendstil**

Designing artist:
Barbara Bloom

Curator: Christian Witt-Dörring

The movie synopsis would read something like this: Michael Thonet, a German chair designer, so impressed an Austrian prince with his elegant designs and innovative manufacturing techniques, that he was commissioned to design some woodworking for a palace in Vienna, and then encouraged by higher-ups to relocate his factory to Austria. There, his business flourished to become a late nineteenth-century international success story.

This is an exemplary case of an aesthetically sophisticated designer who was willing to experiment with production techniques. A man dedicated to reductive methods, in which (as a forerunner for the Modernist's 'Form Follows Function') he allowed the intrinsic qualities of his material, wood, to dictate the form of his designs. He was a reductivist in terms of production as well, sparing materials and time with his economical assembly line; turning a handicraft into an international mass produced industry. He mass-advertised and distributed his furniture by catalogue, indicating that Thonet was also a brilliant early capitalist. He understood the need to develop a consumer society whose needs were *created* and then met.

It's a good docudrama with a clear linear narrative. I'd like to see the part of Thonet played by someone like Nick Nolte, accented, and convincingly depicting his long and eventful life. There would be International Trade Fair first prizes, certainly several Vienna café scenes, and perhaps a factory class conflict. Good plot!

But I really look forward to (and hope I live long enough to see) a made-for-inter-active video-docudrama, which might be made in the early or mid twenty-first century, about the life of Ingvar Kamprad, the founder of IKEA. This late twentieth-century prototype of business success needs no introduction. But in the future it will be remembered as a marketer of great appeal to a wide range of customers; from most European intellectuals who filed their libraries on 'Billy' bookshelves, to young 1½-kid families who were helped over the hurdle of spending money by IKEA's clever tactic of giving every object in their catalogue a proper name. So, you didn't need to buy a couch, when you could bring 'Bjorn' home with you.

So, imagine a double-bill of these two movies. Together they form a good paradigm of progress. What lives on? Is it the self-evident aesthetics and design finesse of Thonet? His dedication to experimental techniques? His reductivist methods? Or, some mutant late capitalism, some anthropomorhised form of supply and demand, in which the consumer need is created by 'Bambi-fication'. I'm sure the IKEA movie will be produced by Disney.   *Barbara Bloom*

Although bentwood furniture was not a Viennese invention, the bentwood chair is still frequently referred to outside Austria as the 'Viennese chair'. The technique of bending steamed wood was common as early as the Middle Ages.

Born in Boppard on the Rhine, Micheal Thonet (1796–1871) was an innovative furniture-maker, and during the 1830s he attempted to develop a technically more econmical version of curved, late Biedermeier furniture shapes. He succeeded, using bent and glued laminates. His move to Vienna in 1842 by arrangement with Prince Metternich opened up to him the much wider market of the Austrian Empire. He continued consistently to develop bentwood techniques further, and in 1852 succeeded in registering a patent for the bending of glued laminates into curvilinear forms, and finally in 1856 a patent for the bending of solid wood. In addition to the further development of bentwood techniques, Thonet's immense achievement lay in his talent for applying these techniques to producing distinctive products whose natural form and timelessness appealed to a broad public. His aesthetic, which developed out of his fascination with a production technique, opened new perspectives in seating furniture.

From its furniture collection, the MAK presents an overview of over a hundred years of production by Thonet and competing firms, from the 1830s to the 1930s. *Christian Witt-Dörring*

Chair
Boppard (Rhine), ca. 1836/40
Design and manufacture: Michael Thonet
Bent laminated wood, solid wood; veneered walnut; cane
Inv. no. H 2967/1987
Formerly in the collection of A. v. Vegesack

Chair, model no. 1
Vienna, prior to 1854
Manufacture: Thonet brothers, ca. 1858
Bent solid beechwood, bent laminated
wood; palisander finish; cane
Inv. no. H 2299/1975

Chair, model no. 8
Vienna, 1858
Manufacture: Thonet brothers, 1858
Bent solid beechwood, bent laminated
wood; palisander finish; cane
Inv. no. H 3019/1988
Formerly in the collection of A. v. Vegesack

Chair, model no. 25
Vienna, ca. 1910
Manufacture: Mundus
Bent solid beechwood, solid wood, stained
brown; cane
Inv. no. H 2186/1969
Gift of the *Bundeskammer der
gewerblichen Wirtschaft* (Federal
Chamber of Commerce)

Chair for the Café Museum
Vienna, 1898
Design: Adolf Loos
Manufacture: J. & J. Kohn
Bent solid beechwood, solid wood, stained
red; cane
Inv. no. H 2805/1985

Chair, model no. 322
For the Purkersdorf Sanatorium
Vienna, 1904
Design: Josef Hoffmann
Manufacture: J. & J. Kohn
Bent solid beechwood, stained brown, lam-
inated wood; original oilcloth upholstery
Inv. no. H 2189b/1969
Gift of the *Bundeskammer der gewerblichen
Wirtschaft* (Federal Chamber of
Commerce)

Sofa, model no. 4
Vienna, ca. 1850
Manufacture: Thonet Brothers, ca. 1858/60
Bent solid beechwood, bent laminated
wood; palisander finish; damask
upholstery (restored)
Inv. no. H 2978/1988
Formerly in the collection of A. v. Vegesack

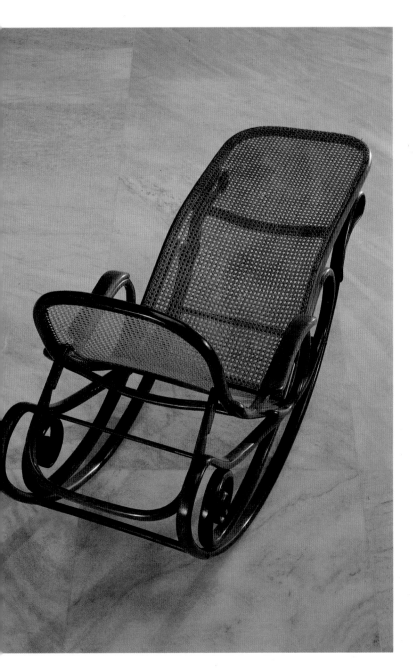

Rocking chaise
Vienna, ca. 1874/82
Manufacture: Thonet Brothers, ca. 1890
Bent solid beechwood, turned solid
beechwood, solid wood, stained brown;
cane
Inv. no. H 2935/1987
Formerly in the collection of A.v.Vegesack

Jugendstil
Art Déco

Art Nouveau
Art Deco

Art nouveau
Art Déco

Designing artists:
Eichinger oder Knechtl

Curator: Waltraud Neuwirth

tradition klimt frieze, macdonald frieze, furniture from 1895 to 1820, art nouveau glass *and present day** a floating display case (23.38 metres long) the glass rooms (each 17.61 square metres) two cardboard walls (height 3.84 metres) the blue box (view downwards)

the diversity of the objects on display contrasts with the equivalence in the treatment of the materials used: naturally coloured corrugated cardboard, sand-blasted glass, display-case lighting filtered by industrial drinking-glasses, a pre-cast concrete element, window frames, metal profiles, glass walls, the view from a wall niche, down into the expanse of exhibition room III

the *glass rooms*: two logical spatial surfaces corresponding to the spatial whole. actually, all that was done was to make the existing invisible spaces visible using glass walls (12-mm securit float glass): size 4.35 metres by 4.26 metres and 4.05 metres high. the glass sheets, arranged in u-shapes, stretch from floor to ceiling. each wall side is formed by three equal-sized single glass sheets. the entrance side consists of only two glass sheets, so that a symmetrical entrance to these walk-in display cases remains. the three glass plates facing the entrance are sand-blasted, and soften the light from the windows to the museum garden and the stubenring behind them. at varying intervals furniture by krenn, wimmer, peche, wagner, breuer, singer, haertl, frank, hoffmann, loos, van de welde will be shown here.

the *hanging display case*: it consists of 6 (7) glass cases, each 3.34 metres long, arranged in a straight row. the display cases are hung from the ceiling with orni profiles and so raise the coloured glass objects that are displayed in them to the observer's eye level. an intermediate level of industrial glasses arranged in series serves as an ultraviolet filter and refractor for the light falling on the hanging display case from above. this shining cross-beam of glass and metal allows the pieces exhibited – art nouveau glassware and metalware – to be seen from three sides at once: from in front, from behind, from below.

the two *cardboard walls* are protective boxes for very fragile exhibits: klimt's werkstätte sketches for the stoclet palace, and 'the seven princesses', a painted relief plaster with semi-precious stones by margaret macdonald. the cardboard walls emphasize an altered relationship with raw materials: there is no difference in the way the materials are treated: even recyclable corrugated cardboard is taken seriously, and recyling and possible reuse ennobles the material.

the *blue box*: a window of blue glass in an existing wall niche provides a view from above into the exhibition room, designed by donald judd. this small chapel is formed by a pedestal 30.7 metres high (precast concrete) and a standing, sand-blasted glass sheet.   *Eichinger oder Knechtl*

---

* 'tradition und gegenwart, bewahrung und experiment' ['tradition and present day, conservation and experimentation']: a sequence of excerpts from the press conference 'transformation of a place' with the director of the mak, peter noever

In 1902 Fritz Waerndorfer, co-founder and financier of the Wiener Werkstätte (Vienna Workshops), commissioned Charles Rennie Mackintosh from Glasgow to install a music room in his Viennese villa, next to the dining room designed by Josef Hoffmann. Mackintosh's wife, Margaret Macdonald, designed the frieze for the salon using motifs of the Belgian poet Maurice Maeterlinck. Since 1916 the room's entire contents were thought to have been lost until the 'Waerndorfer frieze' resurfaced during the Museum's reconstruction.

From 1905–6 Gustav Klimt worked on a frieze that was created for the Stoclet Palace in Brussels (architect: Josef Hoffmann). The frieze was manufactured to Klimt's design by the Wiener Werkstätte and installed in Brussels in 1911.

These works, which were commissioned by progressive art aficionados of the upper-middle class illustrate the characteristics of the era: the Secession sought the dissolution of a hierarchical boundary between 'free' and 'applied' art. With prestigious objects, such as furniture, glass, and ceramics, non-industrial arts and crafts became an accepted part of private households. A programmatic equilibrium developed between the artist (design) and the craftsman (execution). The stylistic elements varied around Europe but the network of artists was closely knit.

'Art Nouveau represents the last attempt by art to escape from the ivory tower in which it is besieged by technology' (Walter Benjamin, 1935). Historicism lingers on in its desire for the synesthesia of the 'Gesamtkunstwerk'; aesthetic comfort is forfeited and the modern movement is anticipated in the effort to find the proper form and adequate material.   *Birgit Flos*

Sliding table
Vienna, 1903
Design: Koloman Moser
Manufacture: Caspar Hrazdil (?)
Maple wood, natural and with dark stain,
solid and veneered; nickel fittings
Inv. no. H 2630/1981
Gift of Gertrud von Webern

Ornamental cupboard
Vienna, 1912
Design: Rosa Krenn
Manufacture: Karl Adolf Franz (marquetry work), Florian Hrabal (cabinetmaking)
Zebrawood and black-stained maple wood, veneered; marquetry in zebrawood, amaranth, and maple wood; brass fittings
Inv. no. H 1397/1912

Armchair
Vienna, 1927
Design: Franz Singer
Maple, solid, natural and with brown stain, beech wood, panelling; painted red; strips
Inv. no. H 3004/1989

Art Nouveau, Art Deco

Vase

Vienna
'Octagonal, bronzite'
Decoration design: Josef Hoffmann
Manufacture: J. & L. Lobmeyr,
Vienna
Height: 14.1 cm; 7.7 x 11.3 cm
(top), 5.7 x 8.1 cm (bottom)
Inv. no. GL 3404 (inventoried 1982)
Gift of Josefine Lokey-Fabbri,
Rome

Bowl

ca. 1913
Marks: Signed Loetz (etched
relief), 'Prof. Hoffmann' (engraved
underneath)
Height: 15.8 cm
Milky-blue glass with *verre doublé*,
cut decoration on raw-etched
ground; on the base, vertical bands
in green that continue on the
cupped part in a triangular pattern,
with green leaf motifs between
Inv. no. WI 1594

Rose-water sprinkler

USA, ca. 1897
Louis Comfort Tiffany
Marked: '01116'
Height: 38.2 cm
Blue iridescent glass, surface matt
in the upper area and glossy lower
down; spangles, fine longitudinal
fluting over the whole surface
Inv. no. GL 1989

Vase
ca. 1900
Three double-curved handles
Mark: 'Loetz Austria' (engraved)
Height: 20.4 cm; diameter 7 cm (top),
10.3 cm (bottom)
Inv. no. WI 15 (inventoried 25.1.1902)
Gift of Max Ritter von Spaun

Putto with cornucopia (summer)
Vienna, ca. 1908
Design: Michael Powolny
Manufacture: Wiener Keramik
Marks: 'WK', 'MP' (impressed)
White clay; white glaze, painted
Height: 37.8 cm
Inv. no. KE 9575

Breakfast service
Vienna, ca. 1901–2
Design: Jutta Sika
Manufacture: Wächtersbacher Steingut-
fabrik for Josef Böck, Vienna
Marks: 'SCHULE PROF. KOLO MOSER'
(stamped in green), Wächtersbach mark
Cup (height 7.7 cm): '3690'; saucer
(diameter 16.6 cm): 'DNK 3690' and
'3691'; teapot (height 15.5 cm): 'CNFW
3686/2'.
White clay, glazed yellow-white and blue
Inv. no. KE 9775

Vase
Design: Josef Hoffmann, ca. 1923
Manufacture: commissioned by the
Wiener Werkstätte, probably in Bohemia
(1923–28, ca. 400 pieces)
Model number: va 35
Height: 23.1 cm
Inv. no. GL 3311

Overleaf:

Waerndorfer Frieze
Detail of the central panel
Design: Margaret Macdonald
Three gesso panels based on Maeterlinck's
'The Seven Princesses'
Executed in 1906 for the music room in the
home of Fritz Waerndorfer
Each panel: 152 x 200 cm
Inv. no. MOL 348/2

Stoclet Frieze
Vienna, 1905–12
Gustav Klimt
Marks: workshop producing the mosaic
Gold leaf and silver leaf on wrapping paper

of various thicknesses, with a grid and various manuscript markings
Part 6: Tree of Life with rosebush
195 x 120 cm
Description: '6. Teil von links' ['6th part from left'] and works' notes: 'Blüthe nicht Mosaik Stengel Mosaik. Schmetterlinge nicht Mosaik anderes noch zu bestimmendes Material Strauch sammt Blumen und Stiel nicht Mosaik sondern anderes Material S' ['Flowers not mosaic stem mosaic. Butterflies not mosaic other material still to be decided. Bush with flowers and stalk not mosaic but other material S']
Inv. no. MAL 226 a b

Wiener Werkstätte

Designing artist:
Heimo Zobernig

Curator: Elisabeth Schmuttermeier

The basis for the choice of colour and design in my mural is the festschrift that was published for the 25th anniversary of the Wiener Werkstätte in 1929.

I did not make any selection from the Wiener Werkstätte collection. The exhibition shows most of the works held by the MAK.

The MAK owns the estate of the Wiener Werkstätte. The wall gallery shows the entire extent of the Wiener Werkstätte archives, parts of which can be seen in reproduction in the exhibition room.

To exhibit the Wiener Werkstätte objects, I have used MAK display cases that have been in use in the Museum since its inception at various times and for various purposes.   *Heimo Zobernig*

Founded in Vienna in 1903 by Josef Hoffmann, Koloman Moser, and Fritz Waerndorfer, the Wiener Werkstätte aimed to adapt the formal aspects of everyday commodities to the changed requirements of a new era. Their endeavour to take artistic account of all areas of everyday life was matched by a wide range of goods produced. The planning and execution of architectural contracts was carried out by the Building Office, and items for interior decoration were the responsibility of the cabinetmaking, varnishing, and bookbinding departments and the workshops for metalwork and leatherwork. Between 1910 and 1920, the product range was extended by a fashion department, by designs for fabrics and wallpapers, and also by the artists' workshops, in which work was carried out using a wide variety of materials.

The restraints of the initially strongly geometric forms used in the objects were relaxed as early as 1906 when these forms became inundated with decorative ornamentation. When Dagobert Peche joined the Werkstätte in 1915, the decorative tendency reached a climax in his extraordinary heights of ornamentational fantasy.

The gradual descent of the Wiener Werkstätte to a mediocre artistic level, unprofessional management, and the poor world economic situation that brought a dwindling in the numbers of potential customers, led together with many other factors to the ultimate closure of the enterprise in 1932.

In 1937, the Archive of the Wiener Werkstätte was offered for sale to the MAK. By arrangement with its last owner, Alfred Hofmann, it was stored in the Museum during the Second World War, and was in the end donated to the Museum in 1955. The Archive consists of sketches for a wide variety of materials by all of the artists who worked either in or for the Wiener Werkstätte, in addition to photograph albums, model books, original fabric patterns, production drawings for embroidery and lace, commercial art, files and correspondence, and much more as well.   *Elisabeth Schmuttermeier*

Writing cabinet for the Waerndorfer family
Manufacture: Wiener Werkstätte, 1903–1904
Design: Koloman Moser
Veneered Macassar ebony, marquetry in Madagascar ebony, boxwood, mahogany; ivory, tortoiseshell; brass fittings
Inv. no. H 2305/1976

Pepper and paprika pot
Manufacture: Wiener Werkstätte, 1903
Design: Josef Hoffmann
Silver, cornelian
Inv. no. GO 2108/1990

Tea service
Manufacture: Wiener Werkstätte (Konrad
Koch), 1903
Design: Josef Hoffmann
Silver, coral, ebony
Inv. no. GO 2005/1965

Casket
Manufacture: Wiener Werkstätte
(Adolf Erbrich, Karl Ponocny), 1906
Design: Koloman Moser
Silver, enamel, semi-precious stones
Inv. no. GO 1397/1908

Vase
Manufacture: Wiener Werkstätte,
1903–1904
Design: Koloman Moser
Brass, citrine ('false topaz')
Inv. no. ME 915/1965

Pendant
Manufacture: Wiener Werkstätte, 1903
Design: Koloman Moser
Silver, opal
Inv. no. BI 1495

Gift of honour on Josef Hoffmann's 50th birthday
Manufacture: Wiener Werkstätte, 1920
Design: Dagobert Peche
Silver, ivory, soapstone
Inv. no. GO 1788/1925

Design for a cupboard
Dagobert Peche
Manufacture: Wiener Werkstätte, 1919
Coloured pencil, ink on paper
Inv. no. KI 8391/28

Festschrift on the 25th anniversary of the Wiener Werkstätte
Wiener Werkstätte, 1903–1928: Modernes Kunstgewerbe und sein Weg (Modern Arts and Crafts and Their Development)
Vienna: Krystall-Verlag, 1929
Design: Vally Wieselthier, Gudrun Baudisch
Manufacture: J. Gerstmayer, Vienna
Binding: papier mâché with relief figures in red and black, 23 x 21.8 cm
Inv. no. BI 18873

The book was produced to Josef Hoffmann's specifications, and was

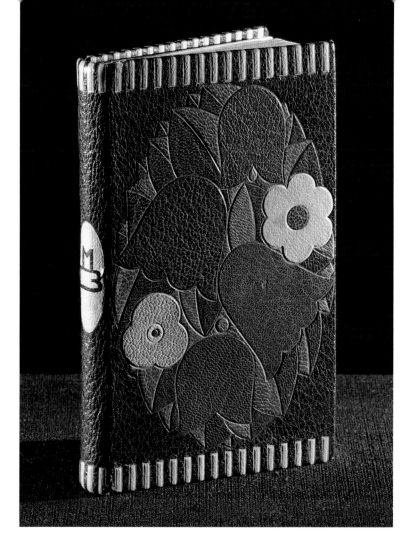

intended to offer a free interpretation of the concept 'arts and crafts' through the medium of book design, an intention immediately evident in the untitled binding with its papier mâché relief.

Bookbinding

Wiener Werkstätte, ca. 1914
Max Brod, *Der Bräutigam* (The Bridegroom)
Berlin, n. d.
Design: Josef Hoffmann
Manufacture: Wiener Werkstätte (Ludwig Willner)
Signed: 'JH', 'Wiener Werkstätte', 'LW'
Polychromatic Morocco leather with appliqué floral still life and strict line ornamentation
14x8.5cm
On the spine, the initials 'MB'
Inv. no. BI 21192/1936

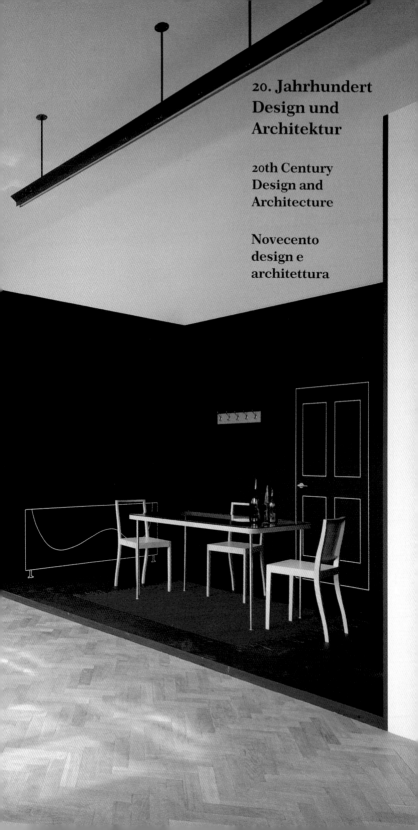

20. Jahrhundert
Design und
Architektur

20th Century
Design and
Architecture

Novecento
design e
architettura

Designing artist:
Manfred Wakolbinger

Curator: Peter Noever

The design area includes exemplary furniture by Jasper Morrison (Britain), Charles Eames (USA), Walter Pichler (Austria), Philip Starck (France), Frank O. Gehry (USA), Gregor Eichinger (Austria), and Italian and Scandinavian glass objects from the 1950s. The architecture area presents models and drawings by Raimund Abraham (Austria), Frank O. Gehry (USA), Coop Himmelblau (Austria), Günther Domenig (Austria), Carl Pruscha (Austria), Lebbeus Woods (USA), Eric Owen Moss (USA), and Helmut Richter (Austria).

Recalling Raymond Roussel's *Locus Solus*, stations with various events are incorporated into the room.

Spaces arise within the room.

Part of the way is the catwalk for masterpieces. Black walls with signs and black floor as a stage for simplicity.

The glass wall promises opening to the outside.

The openings in walls offer a glimpse of worlds, worlds of light, colour, and form, and the material is once again glass.

The buildings, standing on special tables, and the relativizing spaces around the individual models form their own stations on the visitor's path.

Manfred Wakolbinger

Applied art must also mean questioning the relationship between art and function, between art and everyday life.

The works of the architects shown in this room demonstrate and document a point of view in which the yardstick for architecture is its universal character.

No matter how varied individual positions may be, all the architects represented in the collection have one characteristic in common: they are concerned with a new type of architectural thinking. All of them tell us that there is no longer any prescribed path laid out for contemporary architecture. Utopian architectural visions, ideal proposals, projections of a bridge between rationality and manifestation stand alongside projects that test architecture in terms of its social usefulness.

The room installation by Jasper Morrison stands for an interpretation of design – one clearly distinct from purely decorative art – a proclamation of design's position, now and today.

The seating objects exhibited by Vito Acconci, Frank O. Gehry, Walter Pichler, and Philip Starck are not evidence of an encyclopaedic effort, but rather an exemplary demonstration of significant modes of articulation in current design, and at the same time also a manifestation of a specific architectural conviction.

Peter Noever

Chair 'Hole in One'
Los Angeles, 1989
Design: Frank O. Gehry, 1988
Corrugated cardboard, glued in layers
Inv. no. H 3035/1989

Armchair 'Richard III'
Paris, 1984
Design: Philip Starck
Manufacture: Baleri, Italy
Thick polyurethane, Dacron upholstery
Inv. no. H 3080/1990
Gift of the Gesellschaft für Österreichische
Kunst [Society for Austrian Art]

Armchair 'Galaxy I'
Vienna, 1966
Design: Walter Pichler
Manufacture: R. Svoboda & Co., Vienna
Aluminium, plastic upholstery
Inv. no. H 2883/1987
Gift of the Gesellschaft für Österreichische
Kunst [Society for Austrian Art]

Vase
Finland, ca. 1950–60
Design: Timo Sapaneva
Height: 26.2 cm
Inv. no. GL 3529

Bird
Italy, ca. 1950–60
Design: Vistosi (ascribed)
Height: 21.3 cm
Inv. no. GL 3553 (inventoried 1985)

Bowl 'Handkerchief'
Italy, ca. 1950–60
Design: Venini
Mark: 'venini murano ITALIA'
Height: 14.9 cm
Inv. no. GL 3528 (inventoried 1985)

Tulip vase
Sweden, ca. 1950–60
Design: Nils Londberg, for Ørrefors
Height: 49 cm
Inv. no. GL 3571

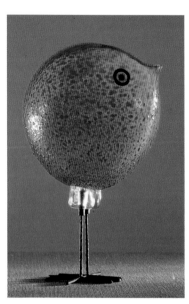

Double Landscape, Vienna Model
Architectural model
New York, 1991
Architect: Lebbeus Woods
Wood, acrylic, metal
63 x 43 x 40 cm
Inv. no. GK 54

Church at the Wall
Architectural model
Berlin, 1982
Architect: Raimund Abraham
Wood and cardboard, varnished
76 x 51 x 26 cm
Inv. no. GK 3

Frank O. Gehry Residence
Architectural model
Santa Monica, 1978
Architect: Frank O. Gehry
Wood, cardboard, metal, and acrylic glass
183 x 122 x 36 cm
Inv. no. GK 84

Gegenwartskunst

Contemporary Art

Arte contemporanea

Designing artist and curator:
Peter Noever

A room for contemporary artists. At the outermost edge, in the attic of the Museum building, linked to the rhythm of the existing exhibition rooms but nevertheless distant, only accessible by its own staircase. A kind of ethereal space, newly created, free of aesthetic speculation and every sort of formalism. A loft extension, a bright, clearly laid out, undivided, open ('work') room. A room to house the gravity, the force fields, programmes, and manifestos of autonomous, individual, universal works of art. Selected examples of current artistic production, torn from their original context, are installed here.

What is decisive is therefore not so much the room as a room, but rather its contents and its alteration, its constant renewal, i. e. the field of tension and the dynamics of objects, installations, and sculptures that interact with one another in complex ways, while remaining individual and different.

An open space, a contemporary space for the art of today. A new spatial and emotional structure that lives on the tension of the works of art within it.

Peter Noever

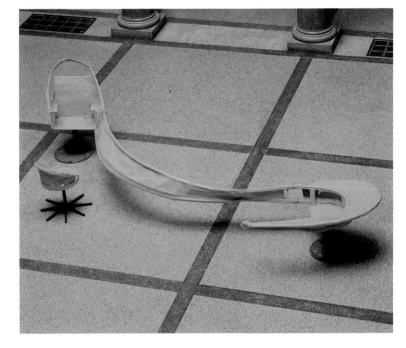

A collection of contemporary art should not rigidify art, but test, seek, and sound its depths. The idea of the founders of the Austrian Museum of Applied Art (MAK) was to promote the arts and crafts, to contribute to the improvement of taste and to act as a model; but today, its main concern is to present current events and products from a specific perspective, to illustrate through its collection the inter-connectedness that arises at the borderline between 'fine' and 'applied' art.

The Contemporary Art Collection, established in 1986, signals an attempt to document contemporary art movements alongside the traditional collections and to face up to previously almost unheard of tasks: confronting art of our own time and seeking a dialogue with the artists.

A start has therefore been made here, in an effort to do justice to the multilayered complexity of contemporary movements, with works by Vito Acconci, Herbert Bayer, Günther Brus, Gregor Eichinger, Padhi Frieberger, Bruno Gironcoli, Heinz Frank, Magdalena Jetelová, Donald Judd, Birgit Jürgensen, Milan Knizak, Brigitte Kowanz, Hans Kupelwieser, Heinz Leitner, Christoph Lissy, Helmut Mark, Oswald Oberhuber, Walter Pichler, Arnulf Rainer, Alfons Schilling, Eva Schlegel, Hubert Schmalix, Rudolf Schwarzkogler, Ingeborg Strobel, Mario Terzic, James Turrell, Manfred Wakolbinger, Hans Weigand, Franz West, Erwin Wurm, and Heimo Zobernig, as well as experimental architectural projects and demonstrations by Raimund Abraham, Coop Himmelblau, Günther Domenig, Frank O. Gehry, John Hejduk, Eric Owen Moss, Carl Pruscha, and Lebbeus Woods.

The appraisal of art in museums, of all places, should never be one-sided, but must constantly respond to the questions and topics of the time. Back to the present means: breaking out of the status quo and provoking questions, in order to arrive at the new forms of perception that are a fundamental constituent of every culture.

The MAK Contemporary Art Collection in this borderline field is therefore oriented towards an emphasis on contemporary Austrian artistic production and works by artists who, through exhibitions and other events, have direct connections with this institution.   *Peter Noever*

Franz West
Eo Ipso
1987
Two parts, iron, spray-coated
546 x 118 x 115 cm; 83 x 57 x 52 cm
Inv. no. GK 16

Hans Kupelwieser
Untitled (Ohne Titel)
1988
Two parts, iron
322 x 190 cm; 322 x 130 cm
Inv. no. GK 27

Bruno Gironcoli
Disc Ring (Scheibenring)
1989
Model for a fountain
Aluminium, acrylic glass
167 x 100 x 101 cm
Inv. no. GK 25

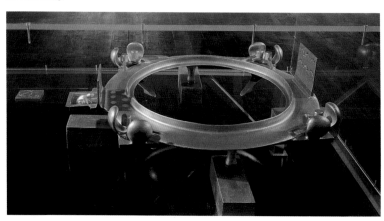

Padhi Frieberger
Material Image (Materialbild)
1948
Wood, paper, metal, textiles
100 x 170 cm
Inv. no. GK 41

Erwin Wurm
Untitled (Ohne Titel)
1990
Wood, fabric
180 x 118 x 60 cm
Inv. no. GK 37

Walter Pichler
Building for Tubs and Vessels
(Haus für Tröge und Gefäße)
1992
Ink, tempera on paper
40.5 x 57.5 cm
Inv. no. GK 88/8

Hans Weigand
Block
1987
Hammer mill paint on wood
125×76×35 cm
Inv. no. GK 45

Brigitte Kowanz
Untitled (Ohne Titel)
1989
Acrylic glass, glass, halogen light
100 x 100 x 30 cm
Inv. no. GK 47

Orient

Oriente

Designing artist: **GANG ART**

Curator: Angela Völker

As a way of approaching the anachronism of carpets hung as if they were pictures, vertical and horizontal presentation surfaces have been produced in the same material, forming a detached unit to provide a 'setting' for the exhibits. The carpets are mounted without individual frames, corresponding to their appearance when in use.

The presentation surfaces are proportioned in relation to the given architectonic parameters, and consist of two units with L-shaped sections running along the long axis of the hall. They are distinct from the floor and walls, and their state of 'suspension' is enhanced by the restricted lighting. The colouring of the elements is a reaction to the dominant warm tones of the exhibits: they are restrained in character in relation both to the carpets and to the architectonic design elements.

The remaining central corridor defines the mode of reception, both by setting the distance from which the exhibits can be observed and by setting the direction of the sequence in which they are observed.   *GANG ART*

The collection of oriental carpets in the MAK is one of the finest, most valuable, and best known in the world, although not one of the most extensive. The collection's emphasis on 'classic' carpets of the sixteenth and seventeenth centuries derives from the former Austrian Imperial Family, whose carpets passed to the Museum after World War I. Examples of these are the silk hunting carpet and the silk Mameluke carpet, the only one in the world to have survived.

In the oriental world, the knotted carpet laid on the floor is the most important element of interior decoration, both in the nomadic period and in the ruler's palace. Artistic inventiveness, manual dexterity, and expensive materials are therefore plentifully applied. Artistically painted and glazed tiles play a comparably important role in the decoration of walls. The panelling boards from the mimbar of the Lagin in Cairo are a superb example of early Islamic wood-carving.

The carpets exhibited here were produced from precise models by professional craftsmen working in manufactories. The format, which is sometimes quite large, shows that they were probably destined only for use in palaces. It is still not certain how the carpets came into the possession of the Austrian Imperial Family, in which they were treated as very highly valued household objects, not as collector's items.

A third source of the collection, in addition to the Museum's own acquisitions, is the Oriental or Trade Museum, whose carpets passed to the MAK when it was closed in 1907.   *Angela Völker*

Silk knotted carpet – Mameluke carpet
Egypt (Cairo), beginning of the 16th century
Warp, weft, pile: silk – asymmetrical knots
547 x 298 cm
Inv. no. T 8332/1922
Formerly in the possession of the Imperial Family

124   *Orient*

Silk knotted carpet – hunting carpet
Kashan (central Persia), first half of the 16th century
Warp, weft, pile: silk – asymmetrical knots, sewn
687 × 331 cm
Inv. no. т 8336/1922
Formerly in the possession of the Imperial Family

Fragment of a knotted carpet – vase carpet
Kerman (southern Persia), second half of the 16th century
Warp: cotton, weft: wool, silk; pile: wool – asymmetrical knots
249 × 152 cm
Inv. no. оr 359/1907
Formerly held by the Oriental Museum

Knotted carpet
North-western Persia, mid-16th century
Warp: cotton; weft: cotton, wool; pile:
wool – asymmetrical knots
540 x 273 cm
Inv. no. T 9026/1941

Prayer carpet
Istanbul or Bursa, second half of the 16th
century
Warp, weft: silk; pile: wool, cotton – asym-
metrical knots
181 x 127 cm
Inv. no. T 8327/1922
Formerly in the possession of the Imperial
Family

Knotted carpet
India, 17th century
Warp, weft: cotton; pile: wool – asymmetrical knots
233 x 158 cm
Inv. no. OR 292/1907
Formerly held by the Oriental Museum

Rosette
Donated by Sultan Lagin in 1296
From the mimbar of the Ibn Tulun Mosque in Cairo
Constructed from 35 carved and inlaid wood panels
Diameter: 132 cm

Tile
Persia, 17th–18th centuries
Ceramic, with geometrical ornamentation and enamel glaze
Inv. no. KE 10563

Ostasien

Far East

Estremo oriente

Curator: Johannes Wieninger

A Far Eastern collection, especially when displayed in association with European art, is a form of Orientalism in itself. All of the art works exhibited here were ultimately chosen by Europeans, either for everyday use, for show, or 'only' as collector's items. A European taste is being represented here in which the centuries-old interrelationship between Asia and Europe survives.

Some of the groups of items shown – such as the examples of K'ang-Hsi porcelain from the collection of Augustus, the Elector of Saxony, objects formerly owned by the Habsburgs, or porcelain pieces with European gold mountings – have been in Europe for centuries, and have had a lasting influence on the history of our art. Others – such as the numerous objects from the Exner collection – were brought to Europe during the first half of the present century in order to present an image of Asia that corresponded to developments in art history.

The juxtaposition of European and Asiatic works of art is a tradition that goes back to the Middle Ages, and one that is continued in this Museum. Even here, there was no Far Eastern Department until some fifty years ago; until then, the objects were distributed among the 'European' departments.

The hall in which the collection's 'highlights' and its abundant materials are shown is a central space around which the study collection is grouped. It therefore forms a transitional zone between the exhibition rooms designed by the artists and the study rooms belonging to the other sections of the Museum's collections.

Johannes Wieninger

Bowl
China, Yüan Dynasty (1234–1368), mid-14th century
Porcelain with painting in cobalt blue beneath the glaze
Height: 11 cm; diameter: 40 cm
Inv. no. KE 2259

Bowl
China, Ming Dynasty (1368–1644), second half of the 14th century
Wood with carved lacquer in variously coloured layers (so-called 'Guri lacquer')
Height: 4.8 cm; diameter: 25.5 cm
Inv. no. LA 220

Previous pages:
Unicorn (burial figure)
China, Wuwei (Gansu), Later Han
Dynasty (25–220)
Wooden sculpture with remnants of black
painting
Height: 36 cm; length: 88 cm
Inv. no. PL 896

Bodhisattva
China, Sung Dynasty (960–1279), 12th
century
Wooden sculpture with remains of an
original base
Height: 162.5 cm
Inv. no. PL 846

Head of a Temple Guardian
China, Tang Dynasty (618–907)
Fragment of a coarse-grained limestone
sculpture
Height: 22 cm
Inv. no. PL 659

Box with lid
Kyoto, Japan,
Edo Period (1603–1866),
second half of the 17th century
Stoneware with enamel and gold
painting on the glaze, signed
'Nonomura Ninsei'
(1627–1695)
11.5×17×12 cm
Inv. no. OR 1024

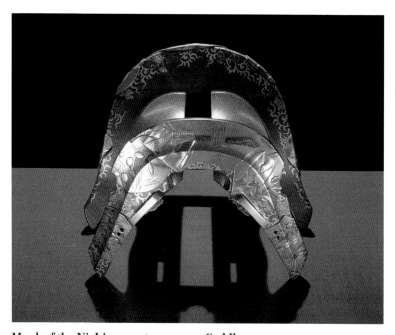

Monk of the Nichiren sect
Japan, Muromachi Period (ca. 1500)
Wooden sculpture with lacquer base
Height: 52 cm
Inv. no. PL 859

Saddle
Japan, Edo Period (1603–1866), 19th century
Wooden saddle with gold lacquer relief on a
gold base, dated 1549, the lacquer decoration renovated in the 19th century
28×40×40 cm
Inv. no. LA 257

Biographies of the Artists

BARBARA BLOOM

Born Los Angeles 1951; studied art history at the Academy of Art; lives and works in New York.
Individual exhibitions include: 1974 De Appel Foundation, Amsterdam – 1976 Artists' Space, New York – 1978 The Kitchen, New York – 1987 'Lost and Found', Gemeentemuseum, Arnhem, Netherlands – 1990 'The Reign of Narcissism', Württembergischer Kunstverein, Stuttgart – 1991 'Signate, Signa, Temere Me Tangis et Angis', Kunstverein, Munich – 1992 'Never Odd or Even', Carnegie Museum of Art, Pittsburgh, PA – 1993 'The Passions of Natasha, Nokiko, and Norma', Marstall, Bayerisches Staatsschauspiel, Munich – 1994 'The Bridge', 65 Thompson, New York – 1995 'The Bridge', The Israel Museum, Jerusalem – *Exhibitions participated in include:* 1988 'Aperto', Venice Biennale – 1989 'Prospekt', Schirn Kunsthalle, Frankfurt am Main – 1991 'El Jardin Salvaje', Fundación Caja de Pensiones, Madrid – 1994 'The Century of the Multiple', Deichtorhallen, Hamburg

EICHINGER ODER KNECHTL

Gregor Eichinger, born 1956; studied architecture at the Technical University in Vienna.
Christian Knechtl, born 1954; studied architecture at the Technical University in Vienna.
Architecture and design: 1985 Café Stein, Vienna – 1987 Editorial office for the newspaper *Falter*, Vienna; Stein's Diner, Vienna – 1989 'Wrenkh', vegetarian restaurant and bar, Vienna – 1990 Helmut Lang Shops, Osaka, Japan – 1991 Truman's chain of shoe shops, Salzburg, Klagenfurt, and Wels – 1992 Redesign of the Roxy nightclub, Vienna – 1993 Design of new offices for the Haslinger, Keck advertising agency, Vienna – 1994 First Floor, cocktail bar, Vienna – 1995/96 Junior High School Peitlgasse, Vienna – *Exhibitions include:* 1986 'Wohnen von Sinnen' (Living from Senses), Düsseldorf – 1989 'Design Wien', MAK, Vienna – 1991 '13 Austrian Positions', Venice Biennale – 1992 Milan Triennale, design of the Austrian contribution – 1995/96 Exhibition design 'mäßig und gefräßig', MAK

GÜNTHER FÖRG

Born Füssen, Germany, 1952; painter; 1973–79 studied painting at the Academy of Fine Arts in Munich, with K. F. Dahmen; lives and works in Areuse (Switzerland).
Exhibitions include: 1984 Galerie Max Hetzler, Cologne – 1985 Stedelijk Museum, Amsterdam – 1986 Galerie Peter Pakesch, Vienna – 1989 Castello di Rivoli – Museo d'Arte Contemporanea, Turin – 1990 'Günther Förg: The Complete Editions', Neue Galerie am Landesmuseum Joanneum, Graz, Austria; The Chinati Foundation, Marfa, TX – 1991 Musée d'Art Moderne de la Ville de Paris – 1992 The Power Plant, Ontario; documenta IX, Kassel – 1993 'Il Viaggio verso Cythera', XLVth Venice Biennale – 1994 'Der zerbrochene Spiegel' (The Broken Mirror), Vienna – 1995 Stedelijk Museum, Amsterdam

GANG ART

Group of artists formed in Vienna in 1985, emphasis on installations and events.

Actions, installations, and events include: 1986 'Gang Art', event, Vienna Riding Institute – 1988 'Fiat!', event, Fiat Building, Vienna – 1989 'Im Nu' (In a Flash), event and room installation at the 'Design Wien' exhibition, MAK, Vienna; 'Limit', room installation at the exhibition 'Land in Sicht: Österreichische Kunst im 20. Jahrhundert' (Land Ahead: Austrian Art in the Twentieth Century), Mücsnarok, Budapest – 1990 (editors), 'Pars pro toto', publication on the treatment of 1950s sculpture – 1991 'Icons', event, Stadthalle, Vienna – 1992 'Die Form der Zeit' (The Form of Time), exhibition design, Böhlerhaus, Vienna – 1993 'War & Transitional, Messages', event, MAK, Vienna; 'Break Even', event, Marstall, Bayerisches Staatsschauspiel, Munich – 1994 'Klang wirft keine Schatten' (Sound Casts No Shadows), installation and event, G. Ambrosi Museum, Vienna – 1995 'Wohnbau Entwerfen' (Sketching residential buildings), TU Vienna, catalogue; Event, Academy of Fine Arts, Vienna

FRANZ GRAF

Born Tulln, Lower Austria, 1954; painter; lives and works in Vienna.

Exhibitions include: 1985 'Un regard sur Vienne: 1985', Strasbourg – 1987 Museum van Hedendaagse Kunst, Ghent, Belgium – 1988 Kunstverein, Düsseldorf; Sydney Biennale – 1989 'Prospect '89', Kunstverein, Frankfurt am Main; Palazzo della Permanente, Milan – 1990 Musée d'Art et d'Histoire, Fribourg; Musée de Toulon, Toulon; Galerie Metropol, Vienna; Galerie nächst St. Stephan, Vienna – 1991 Deichtorhallen, Hamburg – 1992 Galerie Metropol, Vienna; 'Abstrakte Malerei zwischen Analyse und Synthese' (Abstract Painting Between Analysis and Synthesis), Galerie nächst St Stephan, Vienna – 1993 'La coesistenza dell'arte', XLVth Venice Biennale – 1994 22nd International Biennale, São Paulo – 1995 Kunstverein Bonn

JENNY HOLZER

Born Gallipolis, Ohio, 1950; media and object artist; lives and works in New York.

Invididual exhibitions include: 1978 'Jenny Holzer Installation', Franklin Furnace, New York – 1980 (with Peter Nadin) 'Living', Rüdiger Schottle Galerie, Munich – 1981 (with Peter Nadin) 'Eating Friends', Artists' Space, New York – 1982 'Plaques for Buildings: 30 Texts from the Living Series Cast in Bronze by Jenny Holzer and Peter Nadin', Barbara Gladstone Gallery, New York; 'Messages to the Public', Times Square, New York – 1984 'Jenny Holzer', Kunsthalle, Basle – 1985 'Selections from the Survival Series', Times Square Spectacolor Board, New York – 1986 (with Keith Haring) 'Protect Me from What I Want', Am Hof, Vienna; 'Jenny Holzer/Barbara Kruger', Israel Museum, Jerusalem; 'Jenny Holzer, Cindy Sherman: Personae', Contemporary Arts Center, Cincinnati – 1987 'Jenny Holzer: Under a Rock', Rhona Hofman Gallery, Chicago – 1988 'Jenny Holzer: Signs and Benches', The Brooklyn Museum, New York – 1989 'Jenny Holzer', Solomon R. Guggenheim Museum, New York – 1990 Installations in the American Pavilion, Venice Biennale – 1992 Hammond Galleries, Lancaster, OH; 'Selections from the Living Series: 1980–1982', The Claremont Graduate School, Claremont, CA – 1993 Haus der Kunst, Munich; Dallas Museum of Art, Dallas, TX – 1994 Barbara Gladstone Gallery, New York – 1995 Participation: ARS 95, Helsinki, Museum of Contemporary Art, Finland

DONALD JUDD

Born Excelsior Springs, Missouri, 1928, died 12/2/1994; 1946–47 military service in Korea; 1949–53 studied art; 1957–62 studied art history at Columbia University, New York; 1959–65 art critic; 1966 exhibitions at Leo Castelli Gallery, New York; 1986 opening of the permanent exhibition of his work at The Chinati Foundation, Marfa, TX. Donald Judd, an object artist and one of the most important representatives of Minimal Art, lived and worked in New York, Texas, and Switzerland.
Exhibitions include: 1968 Retrospective at the Whitney Museum of American Art, New York; documenta IV, Kassel, Germany; 'Minimal Art', Gemeentemuseum, The Hague – 1970 Stedelijk Van Abbemuseum, Eindhoven, Netherlands; Museum Folkwang, Essen, Germany – 1971 Retrospective at the Pasadena Art Museum, Pasadena, California – 1976 'Sculptures', Kunsthalle, Berne; 'Zeichnungen/Drawings', Kunstmuseum, Basle – 1978 Nationalgalerie, Berlin – 1982 documenta VII, Kassel, Germany – 1984 'Art of Our Time', Saatchi Collection, London – 1987 Stedelijk Van Abbemuseum, Eindhoven, Netherlands; Musée d'Art Moderne de la Ville de Paris; Fundación Juan Miró, Barcelona – 1988 Castello di Rivoli, Turin – 1989 'Donald Judd: Architecture', Westfälischer Kunstverein, Münster, Germany – 1990 Artists' Association, Moscow; Paula Cooper Gallery, New York – 1991 'Donald Judd: Architecture', MAK, Vienna

PETER NOEVER

Born 1941; designer; since 1986 Executive and Artistic Director of the MAK, Vienna; lives and works in Vienna. Since 1975 Lecturer in Design Analysis at the Academy of Fine Arts, Vienna; 1982–94 editor of the architecture journal *Umriss*; 1988–89 Guest Professor of Museum Studies at the College of Applied Art, Vienna; various media activities. Has published numerous books and periodical articles on art, design, and architecture. Since 1971 has been constructing his landscape architecture project *The Pit (Die Grube)* in Breitenbrunn, Burgenland, Austria. Various other architectural projects, including design for the MAK terrace for the Museum garden, 1989 (constructed 1991–93). Exhibition designer in Austria and abroad, including 'Land in Sicht: Öster-reichische Kunst im 20. Jahrhundert' (Land Ahead: Austrian Art in the Twentieth Century), Budapest, 1989. Numerous product designs, some for mass production. Exhibition design and graphic design. Consultant on basic planning, most recently in Havana (with Carl Pruscha) for the Cuban Ministry of Culture. Received the art magazine *Pan*'s Prize for Exhibition Producers in 1991. 1994 'Upstairs Down', individual exhibition at StoreFront for Art and Architecture Gallery, New York; University of Illinois, Wight Art Gallery – University of California, L.A. 1995 Nomination as a juror for Design at the Academy Schloß Solitude, Stuttgart. Chief Curator for the Austrian Contribution to the Triennale 1996, Milan

MANFRED WAKOLBINGER

Born 1952; sculptor; lives in Vienna. *Exhibitions include:* 1983 Forum Stadtpark, Graz, Austria – 1984 Vienna Secession, Vienna – 1985 Trigon '85; Styrian Autumn 1985, Graz, Austria – 1987 documenta VIII, Kassel, Germany; Europalia, Museum van Hedendaagse Kunst, Ghent, Belgium – 1990 Neue Galerie am Landesmuseum Joanneum, Graz, Austria; 'Österreichische Skulptur' (Austrian Sculpture), Vienna Secession, Vienna – 1991 'Interferenzen III' (Interferences III), Museum Moderner Kunst, Palais Liechtenstein, Vienna – 1992 Expo 92, Seville – 1993 Galerie Grita Insam, Vienna – 1994 Museum Ludwig, Budapest; 'The Austrian Vision', Fundacio La Caixa, Madrid

HEIMO ZOBERNIG

Born Mauthen, Austria, 1958; sculptor; lives in Vienna. *Exhibitions include:* 1985 Galerie Peter Pakesch, Vienna – 1986 Galerie Borgmann-Capitain, Cologne; 'De Skulptura', Messepalast, Vienna – 1987 Galerie Max Hetzler, Cologne; 'Acht österreichische Künstler' (Eight Austrian Artists), Kunstverein, Aachen, Germany; 'Aktuelle Kunst in Österreich' (Current Art in Austria), Europalia, Museum van Hedendaagse Kunst, Ghent, Belgium – 1988 'Aperto '88', Venice Biennale; 'Broken Neon', Galerie Christoph Dürr, Munich; Sylvana Lorenz, Paris – 1989 'Das Spiel des Unsagbaren' (The Play of the Ineffable), Vienna Secession, Vienna; Galerie Juana de Aizpuru, Seville – 1990 'Sub & Co.', Austrian Cultural Institute, New York; 'Österreichische Skulptur' (Austrian Sculpture), Vienna Secession, Vienna – 1991 'Transcendent Pop', Trans Avant-Garde Gallery, San Francisco; Villa Arson, Nice – 1992 'Amerikaner', Forum Stadtpark, Graz, Austria; documenta IX, Kassel, Germany – 1993 Kunsthalle, Lucerne; 'Kontext Kunst: Trigon '93', Steirischer Herbst, Neue Galerie, Graz – 1994 Kunsthalle, Berne; 'Jetztzeit' (Present Time), Kunsthalle, Vienna – 1995 Secession, Vienna

In its study collection the MAK displays a major part of its extensive possessions in an arrangement that is specific to the material and technology of the objects, while still corresponding to the specialization of today's curators. The museum exhibits, in addition, are placed within typological, historical, or function-related contexts.

Flexible presentation methods facilitate the display of the various groups of objects in the study collection rooms devoted to individual sections of the collection. The emphasis can, therefore, also be adapted depending on requirements.

The study collection was opened in 1993 with the presentation of significant objects from the MAK collections, ranging from Viennese porcelain to liturgical textiles.

The simple presentation of the objects in a uniform system of glass cases, frames, and platforms throughout all the collections underlines the specific character of the study collection: to promote the clear and comprehensive accessibility of as many artefacts as possible. Its aim is to inspire the public to view things by comparing them. Here, the abundance and richness of variety predominates, rather than individual artefacts.

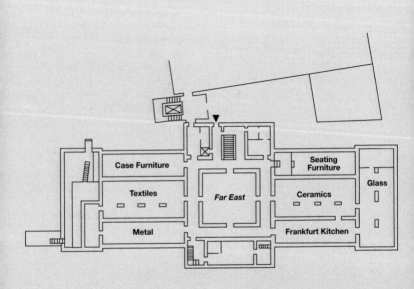

Study Collection: Seating Furniture

Curator: Christian Witt-Dörring

Part of our material memory is located in this room. Is it only a collection of arbitrarily selected household items or is it indeed history manifesting itself here as the totality of our awareness? To what extent do we still relate to these objects in a direct way? Or has an archive accumulated here of has-beens, whose lowest common denominator comprises the classifications 'museum quality' or 'second-hand'? We have the choice between these two associations: between the character of an artefact either as an object or as a function. The latter allows the museum piece to reinstate itself once again as a component of our day-to-day consumer society context. Instead of a one-dimensional history of style we experience a three-dimensional phylogenetic tree of our own cultural history. In the process, the self-evident receives the chance of becoming evident again. This is brought about by means of visually sensuous and non-didactic communication. The visible contrast of different or similar types, functions, stages of development, and materials succeeds in evoking an awareness of the multilayered experience involved in 'seating' and, by addressing the viewer directly, elicits an evaluative reaction that may well lead to a reappraisal of our attitude to seating and how it is so often taken for granted. This stimulation may well contribute to transforming an undiscriminating consumer into a mature and responsible one by arousing in him considerations that have been obliterated by the avalanche of everyday products.

The chair is the piece of furniture closest to the human being. Its proportions are most intimately related to the human body. From the changing aesthetics and functionality of the seat the social morphology of body language can be interpreted. This seems to find expression between the two opposite poles of prestige and comfort, which emerge according to the respective defined values and set priorities. A high, straightbacked armchair demands different clothing and posture from the sitter than one with a low, backward-sloping, rounded backrest. The question of principle arises as to whether furniture conforms to the human body in the sitting position, or vice versa. An extreme example of the latter is the 'Sacco' or 'Bean Bag', on show here, a typical model of seating furniture for the '68 generation. The concept of the suite of seat furniture, which did not arise until the 18th century, entails a number of matching seating furniture types combined to form a decorative whole. It expresses the fact that there is no longer any need to differentiate between the status of the individual users. This development could only assert itself at a time when courtly precedent stipulated a less strict hierarchy between the individual types of seating. In our subconscious, however, this historical development lives on today. As late as 1922, the *Handbook of Good Breeding and Fine Manners* ordained: 'As a lady your proper place is on the sofa, to the right of the lady of the house. As a young girl you should make use of a chair.' Seating furniture unifies the language of forms and of the body into a legible, cultural-historical whole.

Christian Witt-Dörring

Armchair 'Feltri'
Italy, 1987
Wool felt, partly impregnated with thermosetting resin, hempen strings, green mattress in quilted fabric sewn together with polyester padding
Design: Gaetano Pesce
Manufacture: Cassina S.p.A., Italy
Inv. no. H 3099/1990

Armchair
Vienna, 1913
Rattan cane, rattan wickerwork (formerly natural/black-striped)
Design: Josef Zotti, 1913
Manufacture: Prag-Rudniker, Vienna
Inv. no. H 2623/1981
(Gift of Gino Wimmer)

Detail of the **'Chair Wall'**
Various chronological and formal combinations

Study Collection: Case Furniture

Curator: Christian Witt-Dörring

Similar to a character profile, this room in the study collection displays a representative cross-section of the whole range of a furniture collection, thus fulfilling the expectations traditionally demanded of a museum of decorative arts. Analogous to the encyclopaedic 19th-century mentality, to which museums of applied art owe their existence and much else besides, we are guided in our realization of the linear course of history, something that is reassuring. In providing this guidance there lies, however, an effect of limitation as well, and the effectiveness of such support depends in great measure on its 'correct' application.

In the mid-19th century the first historical surveys of the applied arts were performed using methods of chronological-stylistic categorization that are still influential today. They owe their conception mainly to subjectively established priorities, but also to a subjective set of values. Thus, conceptual units arise which are associated with entirely predetermined qualities, on which they also depend. Only when related to the respective cultural-historical contexts do these categories become focused and comprehensible. This serves to indicate the interdependence of cultural landscapes, with their respective functional types, materials, forms of decoration, and workmanship, which take on period-specific forms according to their interaction with one another.

With case furniture, of which there are only a few representatives in the permanent collection, the option taken in this section of the study collection is of a material-specific arrangement. The function of these exhibits, lying in a range between prestige and storage, receives in the process a predominantly categorical character.

As the oldest piece of storage furniture, the chest has been cast in a multifunctional role. It is simultaneously a lockable container, means of transport, and seat. Its emergence belongs to the developmental phase of 'home-living' where locationally fixed households or a functionally specific division of living space had yet to become universal. The cabinet or vargueno, also described as a writing desk in 16th-century inventories on account of its hinged writing surface, represents the typological transition from mobile case or transport furniture to the fixed standing cupboard. Originally conceived as a wall-niche fitted with storage areas, the cupboard has detached itself from architecture and, as a piece of furniture, has become an enclosed space within a space.

Christian Witt-Dörring

Cupboard
Hamburg, ca. 1700
Walnut, solid and veneered
Inv. no. H 549/1988
and
Cupboard
Vienna (?), first third of the 18th century
Walnut, veneered, and engraved pewter
inlays; inv. no. LHG 1411/1971

Foreground:
Sleeping-box for the homeless
Netherlands, 1993
Plastic-coated cardboard
Design: Raymond Voogt
Manufacture: Woningstichting Onze
Woning, Rotterdam
Inv. no. H 3188/1993

Sideboard 'Casablanca'
Wood covered with plastic laminate
Design: Ettore Sottsass, 1981
Manufactured for Memphis, Milan
Inv. no. H 2798/1985

**Cupboard for the studio
of Koloman Moser**
Vienna, 1898
Alder, solid, stained black and varnished,
formerly stained green; copper fittings
Design: Josef Hoffmann
Inv. no. H 2062/1964

The Frankfurt Kitchen

Margarete Schütte-Lihotzky

The Origins of the Frankfurt Kitchen

'During the second half of the 1920s the city of Frankfurt was engaged in a comprehensive building programme. First of all, it was my task to consider the basic principles involved in the planning and construction of the apartments with regard to a rationalization of household organization. Where does one live, cook, eat, and sleep? These are the four basic functions that every apartment must serve. The core function, influencing the layout decisively, is eating and cooking. My first proposal, to build living rooms and combined kitchen/dining rooms, was rejected on the grounds of cost...

'So we decided on a single unit, comprising a compact, fully built-in kitchen separated from the living/dining room by a wide sliding door. We regarded the kitchen as a kind of laboratory, which, because so much time would be spent there, nevertheless had to be "homely". The time required to carry out the various functions was measured using a stopwatch, as in the Taylor system, in order to arrive at an optimum, ergonomic organization of the space.

'The resulting compactness of the kitchen did not allow the use of the standard kitchen furniture of the time, which required more room. The cost savings resulting from the reduced size of the kitchen remained significant, however, so that the Frankfurt Kitchen offered the double advantage of lower construction costs and less work for the occupants. Only by arguing in these terms, was it possible to persuade the Frankfurt city council to agree to the installation of the kitchens, with all their sophisticated work-saving features. The result was that, from 1926 to 1930, no municipal apartment could be built without the Frankfurt Kitchen.

'In this period around 10,000 apartments were built with the Frankfurt Kitchen.

'The costs of the entire unit were added to the building costs and included in the rent, a solution acceptable to tenants because the kitchens no longer had to be furnished.

'On this financial basis it became possible to mass-produce the Frankfurt Kitchen, saving thousands of women a lot of time and effort and thus benefiting their families and their own health.'

From: Margarete Schütte-Lihotzky, 'Erinnerungen' (Memories), unpublished typescript, Vienna, 1980–90

The MAK's Frankfurt Kitchen is a product of close cooperation between Margarete Schütte-Lihotzky and the architect Gerhard Lindner in the years 1989 and 1990. A recreation based on Schütte-Lihotzky's memory, on her expertise, and on her programmatic convictions, this example of the Frankfurt Kitchen occupies a position between copy and original. The original method of construction, the materials (for example, plywood instead of the original solid softwood for the drawers), and the colours were of secondary importance compared to the principles embodied in the 1926 kitchen, with its technically sophisticated solutions, balanced proportions, and a subtle colour scheme that had to be reconstituted from memory.

Study Collection: Textiles

Curator: Angela Völker

The MAK possesses an unusually rich and diverse collection of textiles, whose objects date from late antiquity to the present and range from European to Oriental and East Asian items. Consequently, only a selection – the liturgical textiles – can be presented here, though these are, particularly in Europe, paradigmatic for the art history of textiles, and their workmanship and ornamentation techniques.

Medieval textiles are represented by characteristic embroidered pieces. Their common factor is their creation in professional workshops north of the Alps. The Renaissance is documented by Italian silks of the 15th century, whose patterns hark back to China, where silk weaving originated; the High Renaissance is recorded through costly velvets with pomegranate patterns, also from Italian manufactories. The 16th and the 17th century favoured patterns with small elements and muted colours. This also applied to liturgical vestments. Costly fabrics from the Ottoman Empire and from Persia display materials with large-scale pattern repeats, which were often used for representative liturgical vestments.

The richness of invention in textile patterns of the 18th century is demonstrated in particular abundance through liturgical textiles. The development began with 'bizarre' patterns, which do everything to merit their name. In the meantime the centre of silk weaving had established itself at Lyons, where the following styles were added, first the 'lace pattern', and from the 1730s onwards the 'Style Revel', so called after one of the few textile designers of the time known by name. In the second half of the 18th century the patterns became smaller and plainer, the colours lighter, and stripes and strewn floral patterns dominated until the last part of the century.

Up to the middle of the 19th century an animated diversity of patterns prevails. In the 1830s a special 'church fabric' emerged, which was conservative in patterning and often recognizable through the use of Christian motifs. The second half of the century paraphrased, above all, Rococo-style patterns, although in characteristically variegated colouring, while the Middle Ages were regarded as the ideal model for liturgical textiles. The new products, with their overexact pattern depiction, betray their identity as stylistic copies.

In the years after 1900 the aim was to give a new face to textiles, too. Fabrics from the major Viennese exhibition of ecclesiastical art in 1912 document the new trends.

Angela Völker

Chasubles
13th–19th century

Chasuble from Melk Abbey
England, ca. 1320
Red silk embroidered with polychrome
silks and gold thread, so-called *opus
anglicanum*, linen lining
Inv. no. T 8724/1935

**Chasuble, stole, maniple,
chalice veil, bursa**
Venice, ca. 1715
White silk embroidered with polychrome
silks and metal thread, semi-precious
stones, coiled wire
Inv. no. T 4764 a–e/1986

Study Collection: Metal

Curator: Elisabeth Schmuttermeier

Goldsmiths' work from the 16th to the 19th century forms the central focus of the metal study collection. Secular utensils made of silver, often also gilded, could be used according to function as pouring or drinking vessels, dishes, plates or platters, and centrepieces. Frequently, large and elaborate pieces of goldwork acted as 'prestige objects' on display buffets and, at the same time, as a capital reserve. The history of the objects is closely linked to the development of the eating and drinking habits of the wealthy and their desire for prestigious representation.

A change in table culture also brought about a change in tableware. Some of the sudden transitions in the development of tableware can now be documented only through pictorial representations, for expert opinion maintains that only about 3% of the total amount of earlier goldsmiths' work has survived to the present day. One reason is that constant warfare used up the monetary reserves of rulers, princes, and cities over the centuries, thus leading to a radical exhaustion of the precious metal artefacts that also served as financial assets. Another is the changes in taste and eating and drinking customs, which made many objects seem functionally inadequate and ineffective. Vessels made of precious metals were often melted down, the money invested elsewhere.

The goldsmiths' most important commissions in the Middle Ages came from the Church. Their art was treated as equal to other art forms – architecture, painting, and sculpture. During the transition from Romanesque to Gothic the goldsmiths left their monastery and court workshops and moved to the cities. They now gained commissions, in addition, from the middle classes and craft organizations, such as fraternities and trade guilds. Guild cups or jugs, welcome-cups for artisans as well as for important guests, and presents for legations were all now part of the goldsmith's work. Cutlery, drinking cups, beakers, tankards, jugs, and flagons in manageable sizes were intended for actual use.

In the 17th century, new beverages, such as tea, coffee, and hot chocolate, became popular. Their consumption called for new types of vessel, whose models were to be found in the beverages' countries of origin.

Candlesticks were amongst the most important utensils, having supported the most refined source of light for hundreds of years. Sacral and secular types of candlestick were not differentiated. The majority of church candelabra served secular purposes before they went into the ownership of the Church. It is solely the size of candlesticks that allows any conclusion to be drawn about their function: whether they were used to light rooms and tables, whether they were night lights, or whether they illuminated sanctuaries. Like other gold- and metalwork, candlesticks were subject to the criteria of fashion.

As in other museums, the collections of the Austrian Museum of Applied Arts are subject to certain limitations. Viewed realistically, artistic and art-historical completeness can never be attained. For this reason additional galvanized copies of originals not to be found in the MAK have been positioned amongst the genuine vessels, in order to demonstrate utensil typology. Artefacts from other materials and cultural spheres, which served the European forms as models or were influenced by them, are intended to clarify the cultural-historical development even further.

Elisabeth Schmuttermeier

Study Collection: Metal

Vessels for pouring liquids
12th–20th century

Lidded goblets, bowls
16th–19th century

Study Collection: Ceramics

Curator: Waltraud Neuwirth

The ceramics study collection presents as its central focus selected items of Viennese porcelain, primarily from the foundation period of the Viennese Porcelain Factory. Furthermore, products from other important European porcelain factories, such as Meissen or Augarten, are represented. A selection of Austrian ceramic art of the 20th century, with designs for the Wiener Werkstätte and ceramics from the workshops of Michael Powolny and Hugo F. Kirsch, aims to complete the presentation.

The course of the almost 150-year history of Viennese porcelain, from 1718 to 1864, can be divided chronologically into five sections, each of which is marked by a major personality. Porcelain production in Vienna began just eight years after the secret composition of the porcelain compound, known as arcanum, had been discovered in Meissen.

Claudius Innocentius du Paquier, installed by Emperor Charles VI in 1718, oversaw the manufacturing and merchandising of the porcelain for the first 25 years. Until 1744, production consisted mainly of utilitarian table services, vases, or clocks. The second period, from 1744 to 1784, characterized by the Rococo style, yielding especially high-quality porcelain sculpture as well as scenic and floral miniatures, is termed the 'sculptural period'. During this time the State had taken over the factory.

Conrad Sörgel von Sorgenthal ran the factory from 1784 to 1805, a period distinguished by its superb porcelain painting with raised gilded decoration and use of cobalt blue. Biscuit porcelain – unglazed white vessels or figurines – enjoyed special favour during the neoclassical period. Mathias Niedermayer (1805–1827) and Benjamin von Scholz (1827–1833), the directors of the factory during the Biedermeier era, concentrated on figure and historical painting, Viennese *vedute* (cityscapes), floral painting, and 'leichte Dessins' (light designs).

Around the middle of the 19th century, the production of the Viennese Porcelain Factory appears to have been 'peculiarly unknown', apart from a few outstanding pieces, for example the large-scale floral still-life by Josef Nigg and the series of biscuit-porcelain heads of prominent personalities.

In 1864, after the closure of the Viennese Porcelain Factory, the Austrian Museum of Art and Industry (now MAK), founded in the same year, became responsible for its 'artistic legacy' – its archives.

During the historicist period, there was no independently produced porcelain in Austria. Around 1900 work was carried out mainly in small workshops, or artists' designs were executed in Bohemian workshops. Notable artists were Kolo Moser, Josef Hoffmann, Jutta Sika, and Antoinette Krasnik. Modelled after the Viennese Porcelain Factory, the Augarten Porcelain Factory, founded in 1923 in Vienna, is still in existence today.   *Ulrike Götz*

Study Collection: Ceramics

Items from a service
Vienna Porcelain Factory, ca. 1805
Porcelain, blue ground, portraits painted in grisaille
Inv. no. KHM 269

Cavalier and lady,
***commedia dell'arte* figures**
Vienna Porcelain Factory, third quarter of the 18th century
Porcelain, glazed and partly painted
Inv. nos. Ke 6353, 6352, 4305, 6967, 6855

Study Collection: Glass

Curator: Waltraud Neuwirth

The glass study collection aims to convey a perspective of the development of glass painting and staining from the 15th to the 17th century and of glassware from the 17th century until the present day. The earliest pieces in the MAK painted glass collection date from the 14th century. The portrayal of the Trinity from Heiligenkreuz Abbey ranks as one of the oldest surviving examples of Austrian glass painting. 14th and 15th-century painted and stained glass from St Stephen's Cathedral in Vienna as well as two 16th-century glass panels from Wiener Neustadt provide high-quality examples of late medieval glass painting. As regards secular glass painting, the main examples are of armorial plaques depicting coats of arms, modelled after engravings and drawings by famous artists, which adorned burghers' rooms in Switzerland and Germany in the 16th and 17th centuries.

The MAK glass collection possesses a significant number of engraved and cut glasses from Bohemian and Silesian glassworks from the 16th to the 18th century. Along with these, armorial glasses with painted enamel and black enamel decor were very popular, especially the colourful imperial eagle tankards. In addition, the technique of interlinear gilding – *Zwischengolddekor* – was cultivated. A late master of this technique, Johann Josef Mildner, was active in the Guttenbrunn Glassworks, Lower Austria, between 1788 and 1808.

After 1755 – and especially at the beginning of the 19th century – a reduction in form and decoration asserted itself. The glass artists of the Biedermeier epoch favoured the simple beaker shape with or without a stem. Enamel painting and 'steeping' with mordant tinctures gave the glasses their colour. The 'hyalite' or 'lithyaline' glasses imitated drinking-cups cut from minerals. 'Cased' glasses, made of layers of glass placed one on top of the other, were originally produced in Bohemian glass factories. Famed for their beauty, glasses decorated with transparent enamel painting were created by glass artists such as Sigismund and Samuel Mohn or the Viennese Anton Kothgasser.

The era of historicism aimed to resurrect past styles. Orientation on models from the Near East produced a special form of its own, as demonstrated by the large collection of oriental-style glasses made by the Viennese firm of J. & L. Lobmeyer. If the museum was already a major inspiration in historicism, this tendency intensified still further during the Art Nouveau period. Alongside works by the American L. C. Tiffany and France's E. Gallé, against which the best products from Austrian glassworks competed, influential pieces by designers active in the Viennese School of Applied Arts (Kunstgewerbeschule) and, after 1903, in the Wiener Werkstätte, such as Kolo Moser and Josef Hoffmann, are exhibited. In Art Deco, French glass artists dominated. In the fifties, the Italian and Scandinavian glass industries, with their simply designed, boldly coloured or translucent glass forms, created a distinctively modern product. Venini-Murano and Seguso in Italy, Ørrefors in Sweden, and designers such as Timo Sarpaneva in Finland are represented in the MAK by major works.

Contemporary glass art is distinguished by a separation between glass designers and glass artists. Modern glass manufacturers have established studios where artists are able to experiment with the seemingly inexhaustible opportunities provided by glass production methods.   *Rainald Franz*

Study Collection: Glass

Stained glass
ca. 1370
Two stained-glass panels from St Bartho-
lomew's Chapel, St Stephen's Cathedral,
Vienna, showing The Adoration of the Magi
Inv. no. GL 2227 a, b

Items from a glass service
left to right: two beer glasses, five liqueur
glasses, a champagne glass, a beer tankard,
two beer glasses
Glass, cased in red glass and cut
Design: Josef Rosipal for Artel, Prague,
ca. 1810–12
Manufacture: Bohemia, before 1915
Inv. nos. W.I. 1510/1, 2, 4; 1521; 1525/2–6;
1527/2, 6

MAK-EXHIBITIONS 1986–1995

1986
*Architect Rudolph M. Schindler
(1887–1953)*

*Vienna Construction Sites – Lost Dreams –
Applied Programs*

*Furniture as Architectural Manifesto
(Vegesack Collection)*

Matteo Thun: The Heavy Dress

1987
*Josef Hoffmann: Ornament between Hope
and Crime*

Alfons Schilling: Sight Machines

*Bernard Rudofsky: Sparta/Sybaris. What
we need is not new technologies, but a new
way of living*

*Design-Winter Exhibition 'Schau wie
schön…'*

*Universe in Silk: Chinese Dresses from the
Qing-Dynasty (1644–1911)*

1988
*Art and Revolution: Russian and Soviet
Art 1910–1932*

*Jean-Charles de Castelbajac: Anti-Bodies.
Fashion 1970–1988*

Kurt Kocherscheidt: Summer Work 1988

Günther Domenig: The Stone House

*Peter Weibel: The Mise-en-Scène of Art
History*

MAK Design Shop

The Castle's Kitchen
(Schlossmuseum Riegersburg)

1989
Design Vienna

*Actionism – Action Painting: Vienna
1960–1965*

Art and Industry: Aspects of a Collection

Carlo Scarpa: The Other City

1990
*Hidden Impressions: Japonisme in Vienna
1870–1930*

'Trotz Umbau': Exhibition Series
Oriental Carpets
Viennese Porcelain
*Bentwood, Wicker and Tubular Steel
Furniture from the MAK Collection*
The Frankfurt Kitchen

MAK: Art on the Construction Site

Walter Pichler: Sculpture

*Metall für den Gaumen:
Cutlery from the MAK-Collections*
(Schlossmuseum Riegersburg)

1991
Donald Judd: Architecture

*Aleksandr M. Rodchenko/Varvara
F. Stepanova: The Future is our only Aim*

MAK Winter Exhibition: Design for Loving

Josef Hoffmann: Drawings
(Goldie Paley Gallery, Philadelphia)

Max Peintner: Wings and Fire
(Moscow and Minsk)

*Josef Hoffmann: Ornament between Hope
and Crime*
(Hermitage, St Petersburg)

1992
*Magdalena Jetelová: The Domestication
of a Pyramid*
Installation in the MAK Columned Hall

MAK Gallery
Kiki Smith: Silent Work

*Heinz Frank: What we need is not more out
of less, but nothing out of everything*

MAK Gallery
Edelbert Köb: Birth of Venus

MAK Gallery
Lauretta Vinciarelli: Red Rooms

*Josef Hoffmann: Designs (Ornament
between Hope and Crime)*
(IBM-Gallery, New York)

The Baroque Hoffmann
(Josef Hoffmann's Birthplace, Brtnice/
Moravia)

New Conception of the World and Self-Glorification
(Havana, Cuba)

*Abstract Fabric Design in Vienna
1899 bis 1912*
(Österreichische Postsparkasse)

1993
Vito Acconci: The City Inside Us

MAK Gallery
Pierre Weiss: Dayness

Margarete Schütte Lihotzky: Social Architecture – Witness of a Century

MAK Gallery
*Station Rose: Performance Networking
Cell – FAB 505*

The Abstract Warhol

MAK Gallery
Heinz Lechner: Portraits

Cast Iron from Central Europe 1800–1850
(The Bard Graduate Center for Studies in the Decorative Arts, New York)

1994
Tyranny of Beauty: Architecture of the Stalin Era

Ilya Kabakov: The Red Wagon
Installation on the MAK Terrace Plateau

Mark Mack: Easy Living

MAK Gallery
Rosemarie Trockel: ANIMA

Hans Kupelwieser: TRANS-FORMATION

Donald Judd: Prints

Manifestos: International Exhibition of Contemporary Architecture
(Convento de Santa Clara, Havana, Cuba)

1995
Sergei Bugaev Afrika: CRIMANIA – Icons, Monuments, Mazàfaka

Roland Rainer: Vital Urbanity

African Seats

Geymüllerschlössel

1991
Designs and Drawings from Danhauser's Furniture Factory (1814–1842)

1992
*Eisen. Kunst. Guss:
Cast Iron 1800–1850*

1993
Decorative Biedermeier Fabrics from the Fabriksproduktenkabinett of Franz I.

1994
The Source Materials of the Vienna Porcelain Factory

1995
*Biedermeier in Focus: Designs from the Franz Erndt Stove Factory, Vienna,
1800 – 1860*

Preview 1996/97

MAK
Chris Burden
moderation and voracity (working title)
Austria in a net of roses
Art and Industry
James Turrell
Bruno Gironcoli: The Unborn.
Sculptures

Geymüllerschlössel
Wallpaper from Spoerlin & Rahn
1820–1840

MAK-Center for Art and Architecture, L.A.
The Havana Project. Architecture Again
The Garage Project. Installations by Mike Kelley, Peter Kogler, Liz Larner, Heimo Zobernig
Silent and Violent. Selected Artists' Editions

Opening of the new MAK, 1 May 1993

Carlo Scarpa: The Other City
(12/10/1989–15/1/1990)

Design Vienna (16/2–27/3/1989)

Exhibitions 1986–1995

Tyranny of Beauty: Architecture of the Stalin Era (6/4–17/7/1994)

Magdalena Jetelová: Domestication of a Pyramid (13/5–12/7/1992)

Kiki Smith: Silent Work (*27/5–12/7/1992*)

Donald Judd: Architecture (*7/2–1/4/1991*)

Station Rose: Performance Networking Cell – FAB 505 (21–23/10/1993)

Philip Johnson (left) at the opening of the exhibition 'Tyranny of Beauty: Architecture of the Stalin Era', 5 April 1994

Vito Acconci at the press preview of his exhibition 'The City Inside Us' (17/3–29/8/1993)

Honouring Margarete Schütte-Lihotzky at the MAK, 9 November 1993

Vienna Architecture Conference 'The End of Architecture?', 15/6/1992 (participants: Eric O. Moss, Carme Pinós, Lebbeus Woods, Helmut Swiczinsky, Wolf D. Prix, Peter Noever, Zaha Hadid, Thom Mayne, Steven Holl)

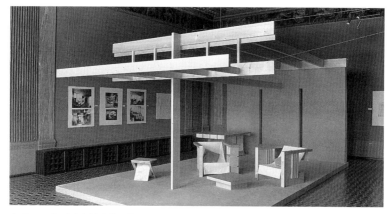

Architect Rudolph M. Schindler (20/3–20/4/1986)

Rosemarie Trockel: ANIMA (11/5–2/10/1994)

Hans Kupelwieser: TRANS-FORMATION (28/9/1994–29/1/1995)

Aleksandr M. Rodchenko/Varvara F. Stepanova: The Future is our only Aim (2/5–31/7/1991)

The Geymüllerschlössel

The so-called *Geymüllerschlössel* is a 'summerhouse' that was built in Pötzleinsdorf, one of the suburbs of Vienna, after 1808. Named after its builder and first owner, the Viennese merchant and banker Johann Jakob Geymüller (1760–1834), the building's architectural language shows the mixture of Gothic, Indian, and Arabic stylistic elements that was then customary, especially in summerhouses. The name of the architect is still not known.

After a varied history, the building was donated to the Republic of Austria by its last owner, Dr Franz Sobek, and became a branch of the MAK. Along with the building itself, Dr Sobek also donated his important collection of old Viennese clocks (160 items) dating from 1760 to the second half of the 19th century. Seen alongside furnishings from the period 1800–40, also purchased by Franz Sobek, which are complemented by Empire and Biedermeier furniture from the MAK, the collection is one of the most important sights in the Geymüllerschlössel. Renovations during recent years have restored the façade and parts of the interior painting to their original state. The subsequent rearrangement of the furnishings and clocks in the various rooms of the Schlössel allows the visitor to view an example of an Empire and Biedermeier summerhouse. Particular attention was given to the textile fittings used in the building and for the furniture, so that the Geymüllerschlössel is today the only place in Austria that offers an accurate and original impression of the variety of Biedermeier interior decoration.

On the ground floor of the Geymüllerschlössel, exhibition rooms have been adapted, in addition to the display rooms, to show annually rotating topical exhibitions that make it possible to deepen one's knowledge of the art and handicrafts of the first half of the 19th century. The Austrian artist Hubert Schmalix has created a concrete sculpture for the garden of the Geymüllerschlössel that will be installed there in 1996.

Room in the Geymüllerschlössel

MAK Center for Art and Architecture, L.A.

The MAK Center for Art and Architecture, a new institution, aims for a radical contemporary orientation. Its program, concentrates on new spatial and architectural trends and developments emanating from the interface of art and architecture – that is, from the complementary and contradictory elements involved in the concepts and methods employed by artists and architects. As part of the MAK Schindler Initiative, the MAK Center for Art and Architecture is dedicated to propagating the spirit of the life's work of Rudolph M. Schindler (1887–1953), the Vienna architect and student of Otto Wagner who emigrated to the USA in 1914.

The MAK Center for Art and Architecture opened its doors at two locations in Los Angeles in December 1995. The architect's own house, built on Kings Road, West Hollywood, in 1921–22, serves as the public centre of the MAK Schindler Initiative. A social idealist and experimental architect, Rudolph M. Schindler developed a model design with regard to ground-plan and spatial quality that was, and is, a forerunner of a new understanding of architecture. The Pearl M. Mackey House (1939) has been purchased by the Republic of Austria and, in collaboration with the Ministry of Education and the Arts (BMUK) and the Ministry of Science and Research (BMWF), has been set up as the first permanent residential centre for Austrian artists and architecture students on scholarships or occupying artist-in-residence posts.

Both buildings were comprehensively renovated and adapted before being run by the MAK as the MAK Center for Art and Architecture in co-operation with the Los Angeles-based organization FOSH (Friends of the Schindler House).

The Schindler House is open to the public as a museum with its own bookshop and archive devoted to contemporary experimental art and architecture, and as a research, exhibition, and meetings centre. Lectures, presentations,

Schindler House, exterior view

Pearl Mackey House, exterior view

seminars, collections, workshops, and discussions, as well as the dissemination of information through small-scale, carefully targeted publications and other media, are all part of the program.

In this way the MAK Schindler Initiative intends to be active in two interacting spheres of the promotion of art and architecture: on the one hand, through the sponsorship of individual artists and architects in the scholarship program and, on the other, through public, internationally relevant activities and impulses in the exhibition and events calendar of the Schindler House.

Schindler House, interior view of Pauline Schindler's living room

Pearl Mackey House, interior view of penthouse

The Library of the MAK

Like the Museum as a whole, the Library of the MAK originates – in its tasks, its intentions, and the core of its holdings – in the initiative and personal commitment of its founder and first Director, Rudolf von Eitelberger (1817–85). The Library was of special significance in the collections of the 'Royal and Imperial Austrian Museum of Art and Industry', which were intended to provide examples and patterns to be used in the improvement of the technical and aesthetic quality of Austrian industrial and commercial products. As Rudolf von Eitelberger envisioned the library, it was to include not only general historical and contemporary works on art history and arts and crafts, but also graphic designs and patterns by artists and craftsmen of all periods and areas. Since the Museum's foundation in 1864, a specialist arts and crafts library that is today unique in Europe has been created to meet this task, based on an original core of holdings from Eitelberger's own private library.

The Library is divided into separate departments arranged according to subject, broadly corresponding to the subject materials and areas of interest in the collections of the Museum itself. With a total of over 150,000 volumes, the Library provides materials on every subject in the arts and crafts field.

The historical holdings are of particular value: manuscripts, incunabula, and tract literature from the Renaissance to the nineteenth century, pattern-books for every area of arts and crafts. In addition to the rich holdings of books and periodicals, the collection of ca. 500,000 art prints also forms part of the Library. This collection of graphics includes an internationally significant collection of ornamental engravings from the fifteenth to the eighteenth centuries, a collection of pattern sheets (from the Vienna Porcelain Manufactory, for example), an important collection of nineteenth-century style copies, a collection of Japanese coloured woodcuts, and a unique treasure in the Indo-Persian miniatures of the 'Hamza' novel. In addition, there are drawings, watercolours, and plans by artists and architects from the Historicist period to the present, as well as collections of posters and photographs.

In recent years, particularly intense scholarly attention has been devoted to the holdings of drawings from the archive of the famous 'Wiener Werkstätte' (Vienna Workshops), which closed in 1932. The greater part of the archive is now held by the MAK. The emphasis in systematic additions being made to the book holdings today lies in the fields of architecture, contemporary art, and design.

Following alterations to the Museum building, the Library now enjoys air-conditioned storage rooms. A new reading room, created by the construction of a ceiling, gives interested visitors to the Museum an opportunity to use the Library's wealth of materials. The room's interior decoration is by Ursula Aichwalder and Hermann Strobl. The former reading room is to be used for Library exhibitions, as well as for general graphics exhibitions. As a whole, the Library is intended to function as a lively communications centre.

New Reading Room of the MAK Library (Design: Ursula Aichwalder, Hermann Strobl)

MAK Works on Paper Room

With the creation of a new reading room in the process of reconstructing the MAK it became possible to use the library's old reading room as an exhibition space (design: Michael Embacher). By means of newly installed rails with movable frames that can be turned into showcases, and with glazed display surfaces in the doors of the bookcases, the room was adapted to house small exhibitions devoted to book design and the graphic arts. Apart from being used to display various parts of the museum's own collection of works on paper, the room will also host touring exhibitions of graphics and photography.

MAK Works on Paper Room
Opening of the exhibition 'Der Relieffries Margaret Macdonalds für den Musiksalon des Hauses Fritz Waerndorfer – Geschichte und Restaurierung' (26/10/1994 – 31/1/1995)

MAK Lecture Hall

MAK Café

The MAK Café by Herrmann Czech, opened in 1993 as part of the MAK's policy of increased accessibility, can be entered from the museum and from the Ring. In the summer months it also provides open-air café service in the museum garden.
Entrance: Stubenring 5
Opening times: daily 10 a. m. – midnight, closed Mondays
Tel. 71401 21 & 20

MAK Design Shop

The MAK Design Shop by Michael Embacher, 1992, is intended to be a central aspect of the MAK's interaction with contemporary design, items of which are on sale in the 80 sq. m. of shop space alongside the products of the MAK Design range and selected artists' special editions.
Entrance: Weiskirchnerstrasse 3
Opening times as for the museum
Tel. 711 36/228

MINERVA Bookshop
at the MAK

On a floor space of 30 sq. m. Sepp Müller created space for the MAK Bookshop in 1992, using several mezzanine floors extending over a height of 12 metres. The entrance area of the store is formed by the 'Gate to the Ring' of the New York artists' group SITE/James Wines. The MINERVA Bookshop at the MAK specializes in publications on contemporary art, architecture, and design.
Entrance: Stubenring 5
Opening times as for the museum
Tel. 33024 15/155

Interfacedesign
MAK Design Service Terminal

MAK Design Info Pool

The emphasis of the Design Info Pool is on the analogue and digital documentation of contemporary Austrian design, along with design institutions, promotion, and education. Information from the picture and text database is available to visitors via the Design Service Terminal. Personal assistance is provided for designers and the general public during the opening times of the archive.
Entrance: Stubenring 5
Opening times as for the museum
Tel. 711 36/320 & 305

MAK Depository for Contemporary Art in the Gefechtsturm Arenbergpark

Vienna 3

MAK Depository for Contemporary Art in the Gefechtsturm Arenbergpark

With a total floor space of 1,400 sq.m., two storeys of the Gefechtsturm in Arenbergpark provide an ideal storage and exhibition space for installations that, created by internationally renowned artists for their exhibitions at the MAK, have become part of the museum's permanent collection. Works of this kind by, for example, Heinz Frank and Hans Kupelwieser, as well as the construction designed by Russian artist Ilya Kabakov for the MAK 'Terrace Plateau', have been set up in the Gefechtsturm. It also houses other items from the MAK's collection of contemporary art – objects by Kiki Smith, Uli Aigner, and Vito Acconci, together with numerous limited-edition series by Rebecca Horn, Fischli/Weiss, Mike Kelley, James Turrell, etc.

The decision to adapt the Gefechtsturm to this double purpose of storage and display was taken because the storage area created under the museum garden during reconstruction of the MAK (total usable floor space: 3,400 sq.m.) proved inadequate to the demands of an efficiently run modern museum. This underground space provides room for storing neither exhibition accessories nor the large-scale objects by contemporary artists that the museum has acquired in recent years. Continuing its original dual function of providing protection and defence in a contemporary context, the Gefechtsturm (which, despite its controversial nature, is inextricably linked to the architectural history of Vienna) now houses exceptional works of contemporary art.

Guided tours of the important section of the MAK's collection of contemporary art housed in the Gefechtsturm can be arranged for groups by special appointment.

Donald Judd, Stage Set

Information

MAK – Austrian Museum of Applied Arts
Stubenring 5, 1010 Vienna, Austria
Tel. (+1) 711 36-0, Fax (+1) 713 10 26, Telex 113575 kunst a
Recorded information on exhibitions and current program: (+1) 712 8000
Press office: (+1) 711 36/233
Guided tours (information and appointments): (+1) 711 36/298

Executive and Artistic Director: Peter Noever
Administrators and Curators of the MAK: Jessica Beer (Publications Editor), Hanna Egger (Vice-Director, Library and Collection of Works on Paper), Verena Formanek (Design, and Exhibitions), Rainald Franz (Library and Collection of Works on Paper), Ludwig Neustifter (Restoration), Waltraud Neuwirth (Glass and Ceramics), Elisabeth Schmuttermeier (Metalwork and Wiener Werkstätte), Manfred Trummer (Restoration), Angela Völker (Textiles), Christina Werner (Press office), Johannes Wieninger (Islamic and Far Eastern Art), Christian Witt-Dörring (Furniture), Daniela Zyman (Exhibitions and Special Projects), Monika Edlbacher (Administration), Irmtraut Hasenlechner (Private Sector Activities), Ursula Hartmann (Marketing – Private Sector; Austrian Art Society)

Opening times
Daily 10 a.m. – 6 p.m., Thursday 10 a.m. – 9 p.m. Closed Mondays
Open 10 a.m. – 6 p.m. Easter Monday and Whit Monday; 24 and 31 December
10 a.m. – 3 p.m.; closed 1 January, 1 May, 1 November, 25 December

MAK Library: Entrance: Stubenring 5
Opening times as for the museum

MAK Design Shop: Entrance: Weiskirchnerstrasse 3
Opening times as for the museum, Tel. 711 36/228

MAK Design Info Pool: Entrance: Stubenring 5
Opening times as for the museum, Tel. 711 36/305, 320

Bookshop Minerva at the MAK: Entrance: Stubenring 5
Opening times as for the museum, Tel.: 330 24 15/155

MAK Café: Entrance: Stubenring 5
Open daily 10 a.m. – midnight, closed Mondays, Tel. 714 01 21, 20

Admission: öS 90 (öS 30 when no exhibition is showing)
Reduced admission for schoolchildren, students, senior citizens over 60, groups of ten or more: öS 45 (öS 15 when no exhibition is showing)
Parents with children under 10: öS 150 (öS 50 when no exhibiton is showing)
Free admission for children under 10; students of the College of Applied Art, Vienna; members of the Austrian Art Society; holders of the ICOM pass; the unemployed; Austrian schoolclasses; and on 14 April (birthday of Rudolf von Eitelberger, the founder and first director of the museum), 10 October (national holiday), 4 November (opening of the museum building, 1871), 24 December, and on International Museum Day (variable)

Geymüllerschlössel, Sobek Collection
Branch of the MAK, Khevenhüllerstrasse 2, Vienna 18, Tel. 47 93 139
(terminus 41, bus 41 A, one stop)
Opening times: 1 March to 30 November, Thursday – Sunday and holidays 10 a.m. –
5 p.m., closed Monday – Wednesday
Admission: öS 30/öS 15

Current information is available in the MAK program of exhibitions and events

While careful attention was paid to the historic architecture of the building during reconstruction of the museum, the needs of the physically handicapped were also taken into account. All rooms housing both the permanent collection and temporary exhibitions are accessible by lift. A wheelchair is available on loan. Handicapped visitors are asked to use the staff entrance in Weiskirchnerstrasse.